I0476950

The Efflorescent Tarot
Coloring Book

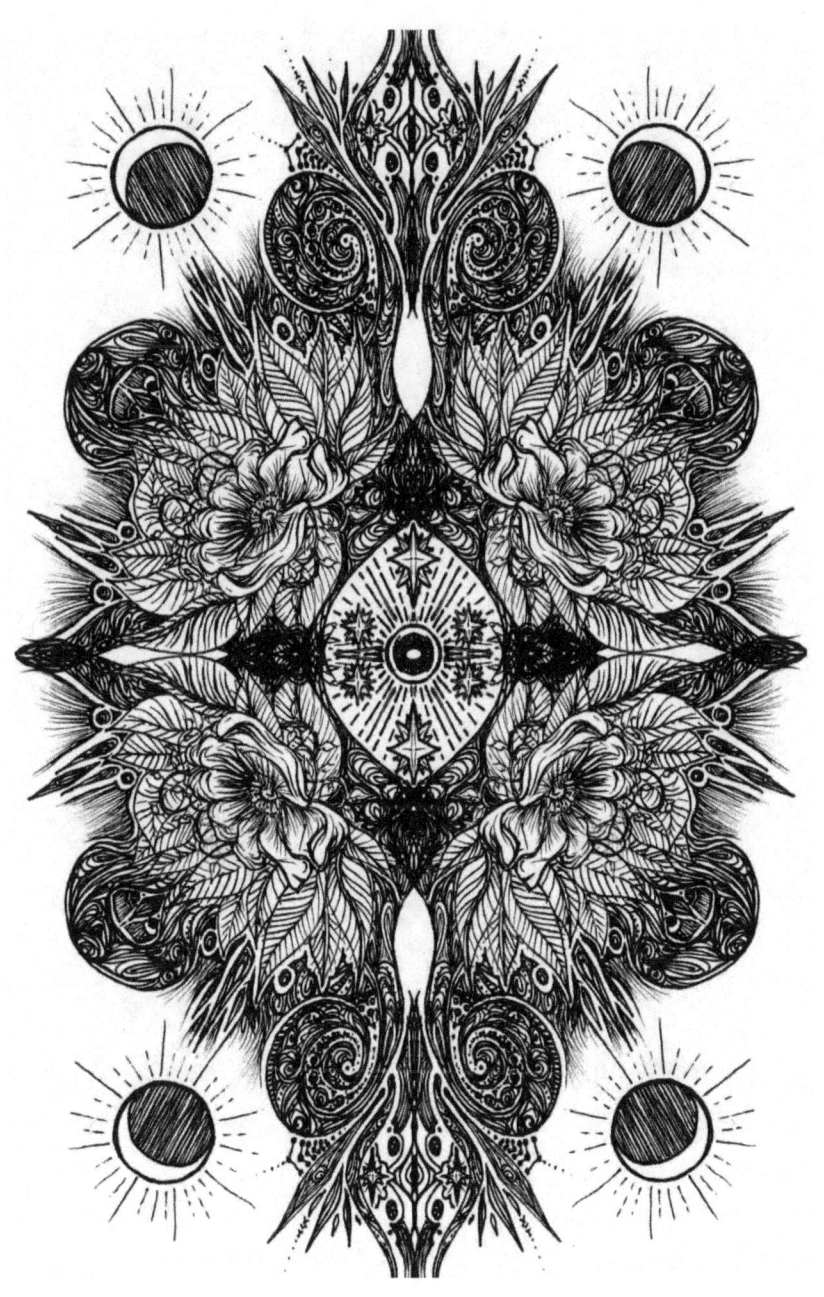

Peony Coin Archer

About The Efflorescent Tarot

Originally drawn over a period of 2 years, between 2009 and 2011, The Efflorescent (adj; bursting into flower) Tarot is illustrated in the Rider-Waite tradition. Like all myths and fables, the deck provides a marginal space between a real world and an interior landscape.

There are many benefits to the kind of slow study that coloring can provide; perhaps it is a chance to learn the stories of each card, or perhaps it can serve as a meditation. Or maybe it is simply a chance to relax into another story, or to have fun. Whatever your intentions are with this coloring book, I hope it serves them well!

Although the best way to interpret Tarot is always the one that works for you, any material that describes card meanings for traditional decks will apply to this one.

Happy coloring!

Peony Coin Archer
Illustrator

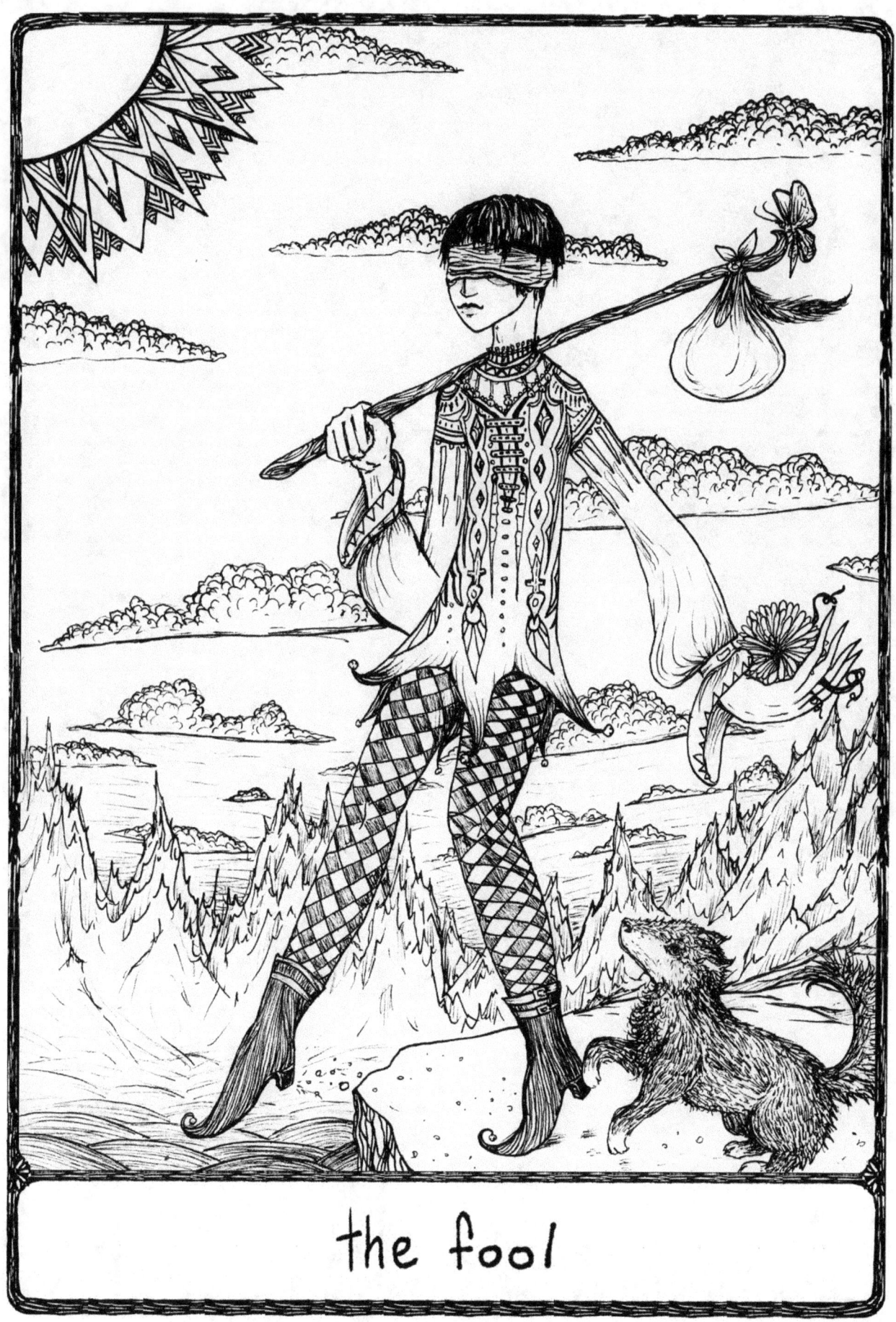

the fool

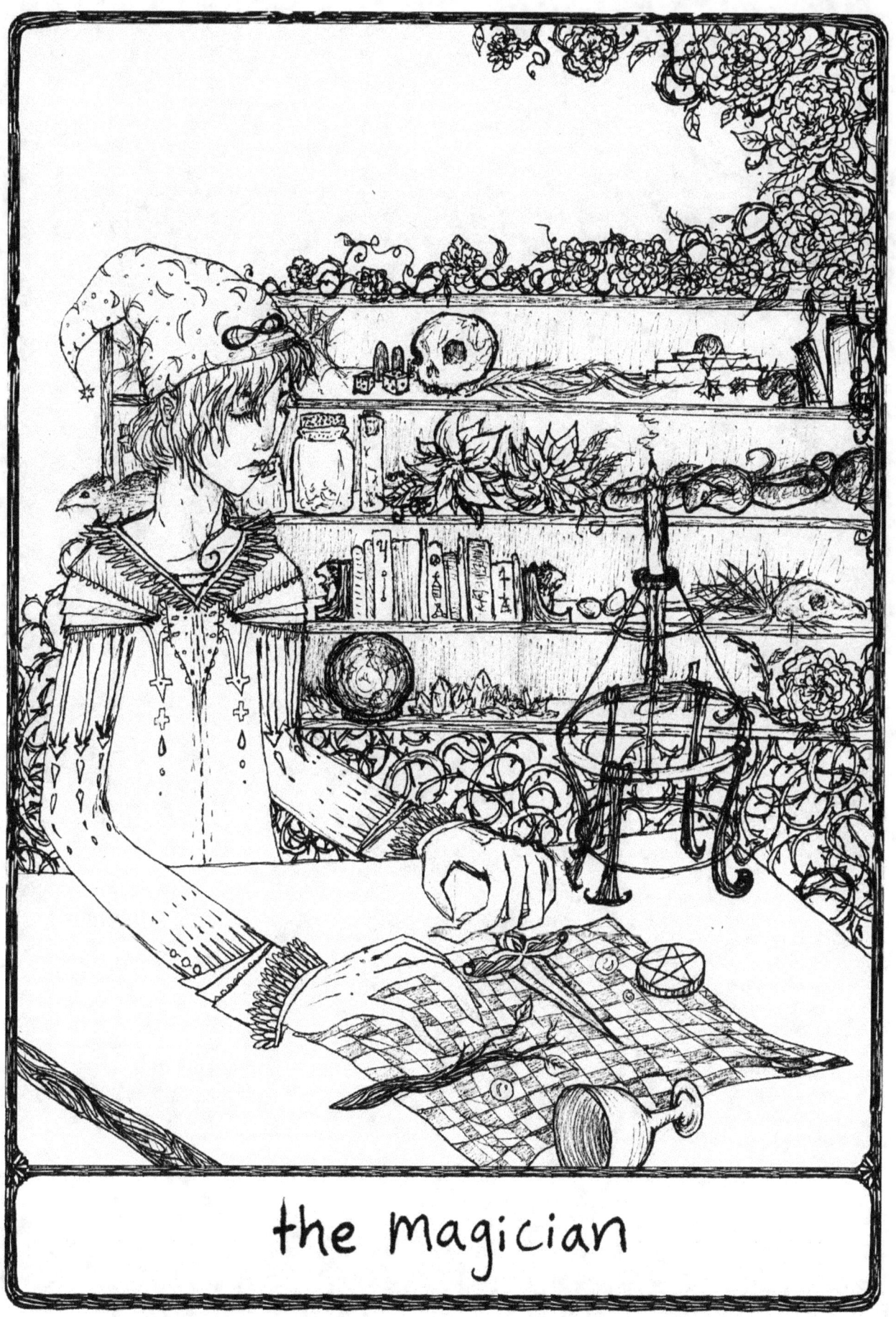

the magician

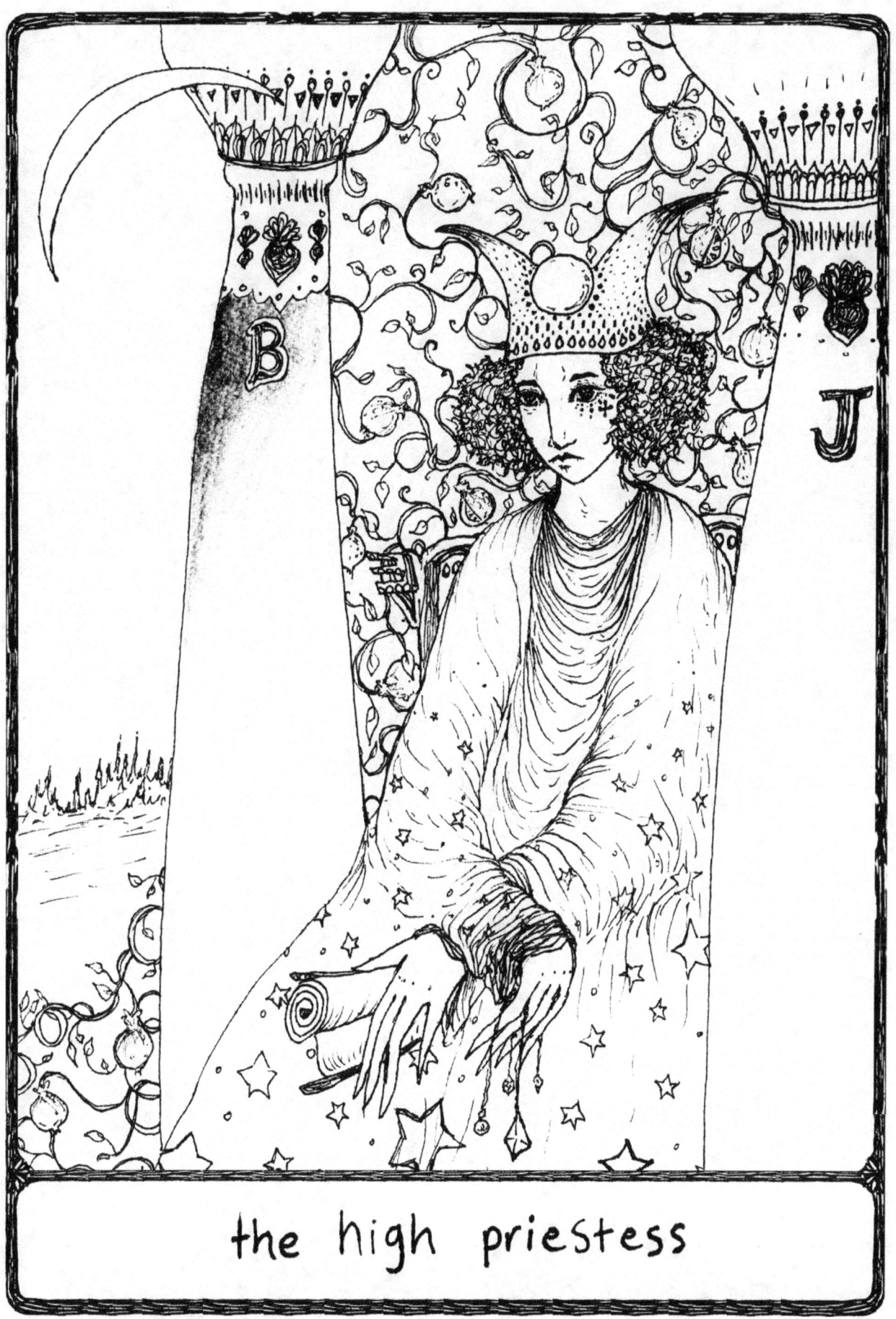

the high priestess

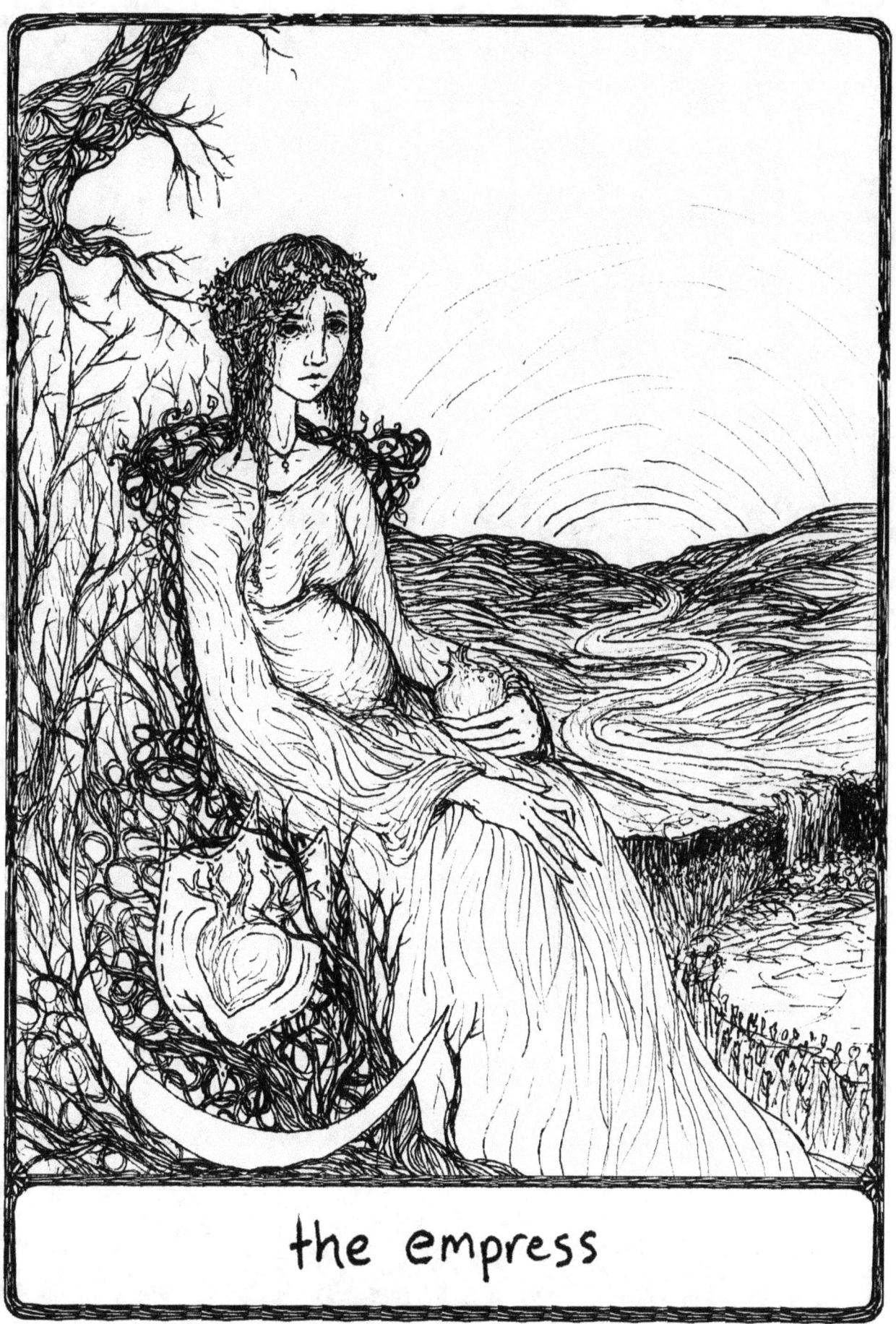

the empress

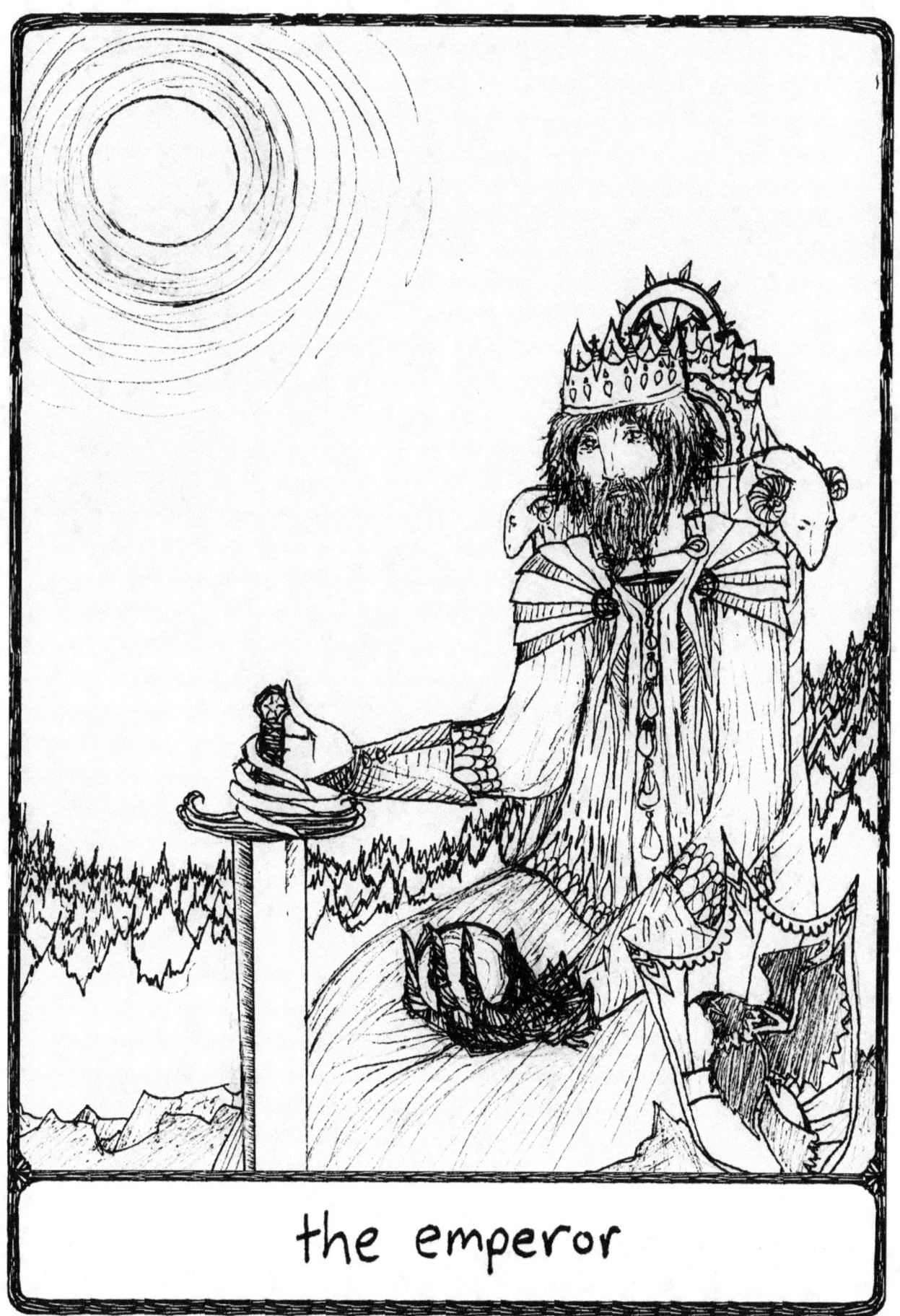

the emperor

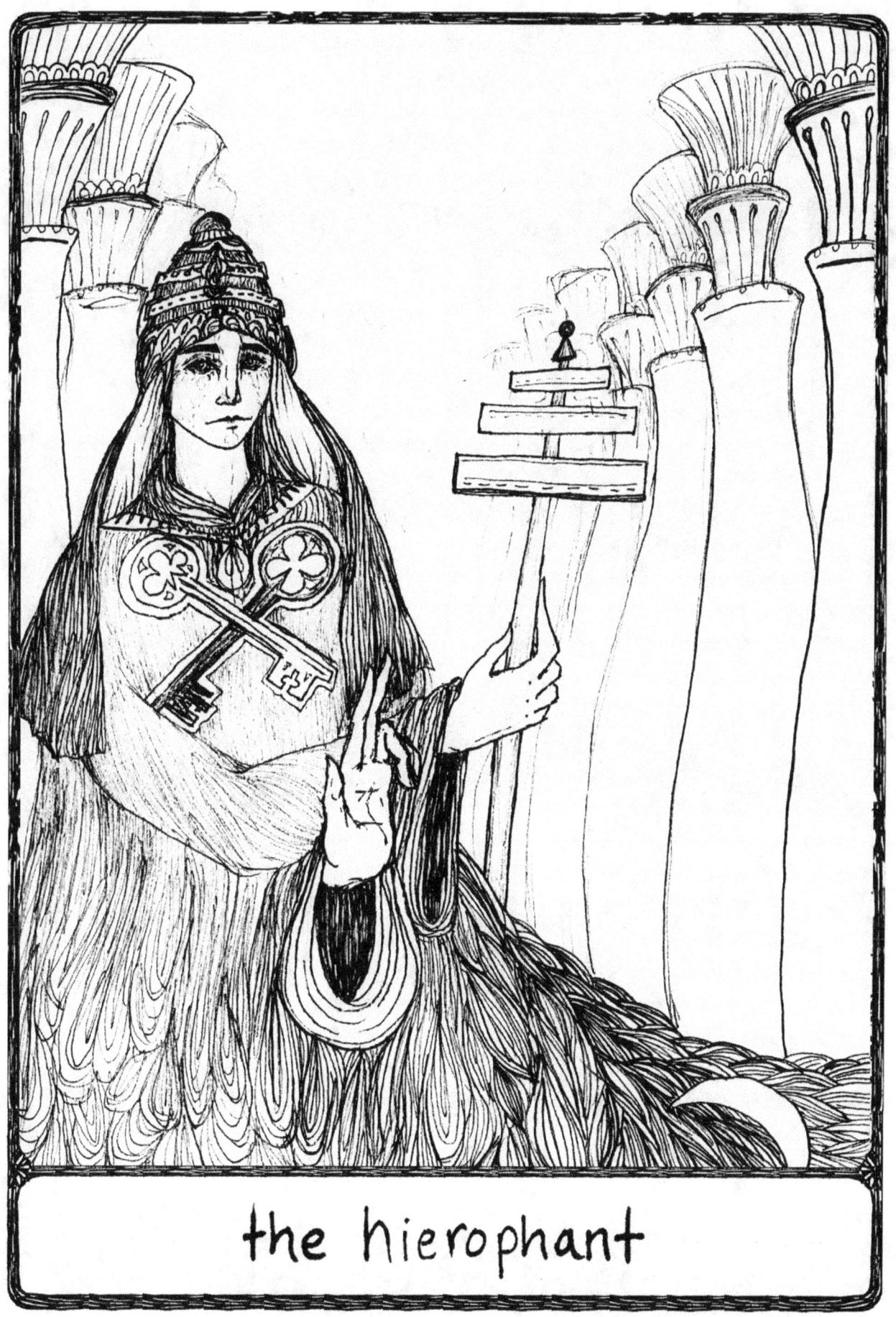

the hierophant

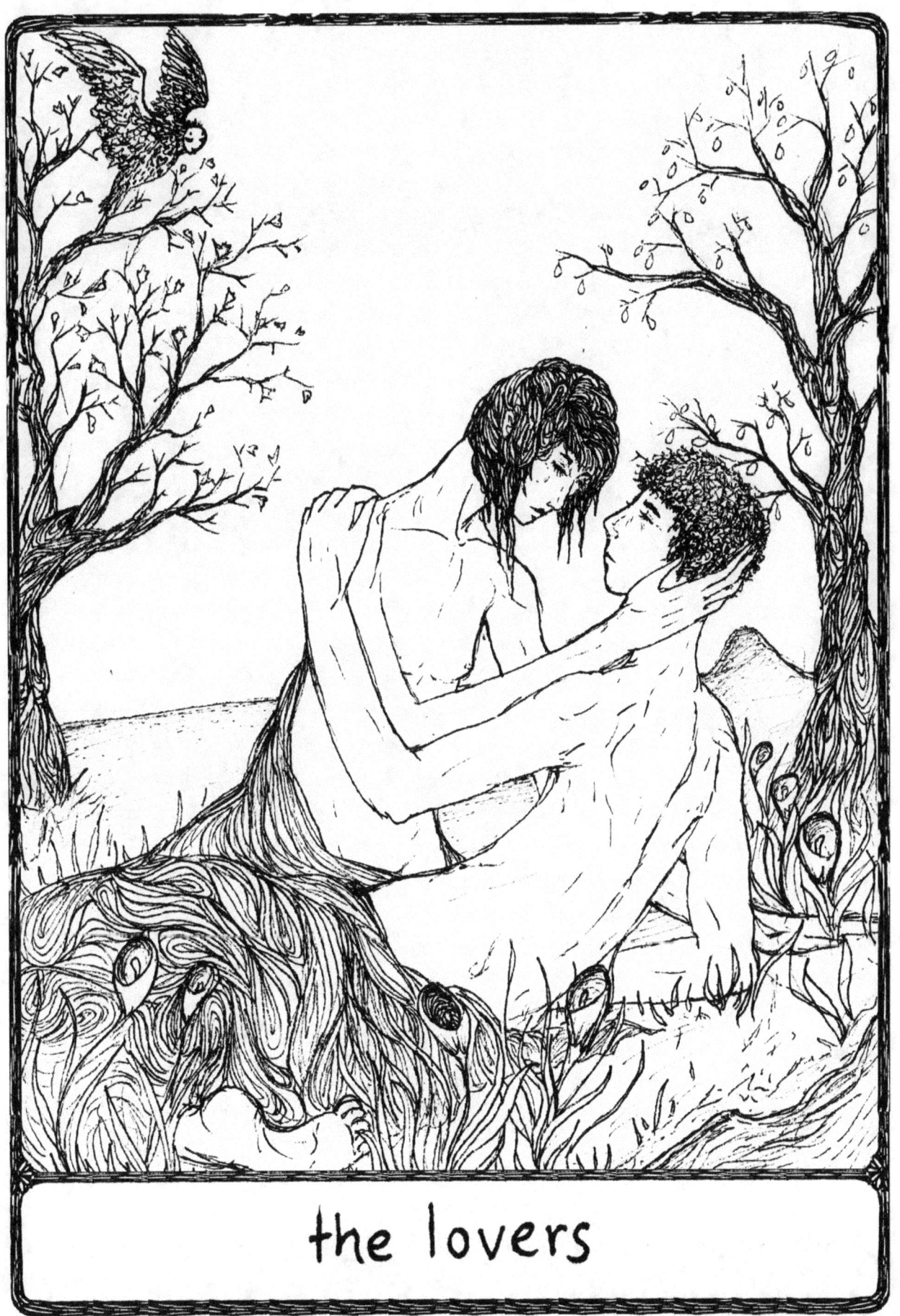

the lovers

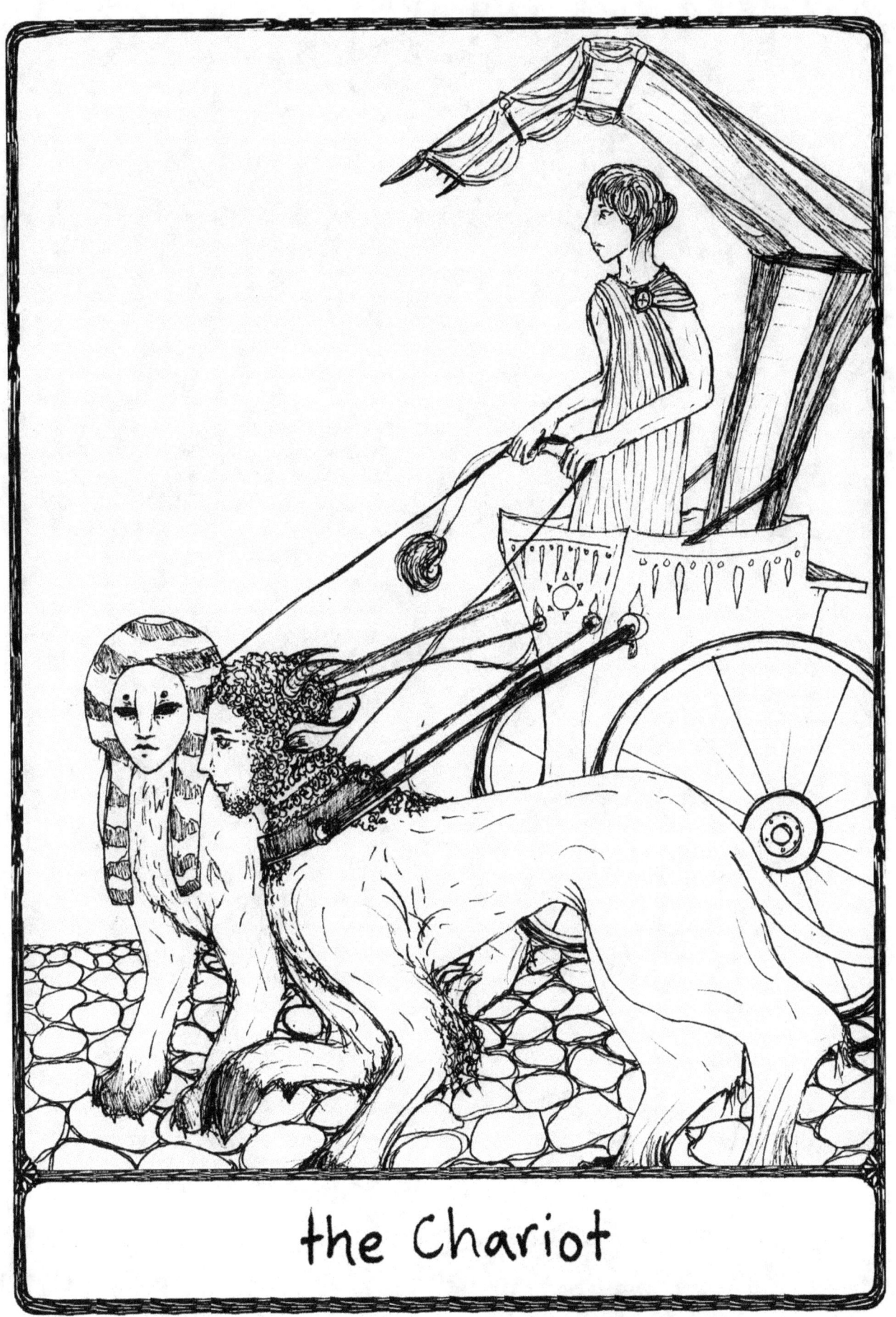

the Chariot

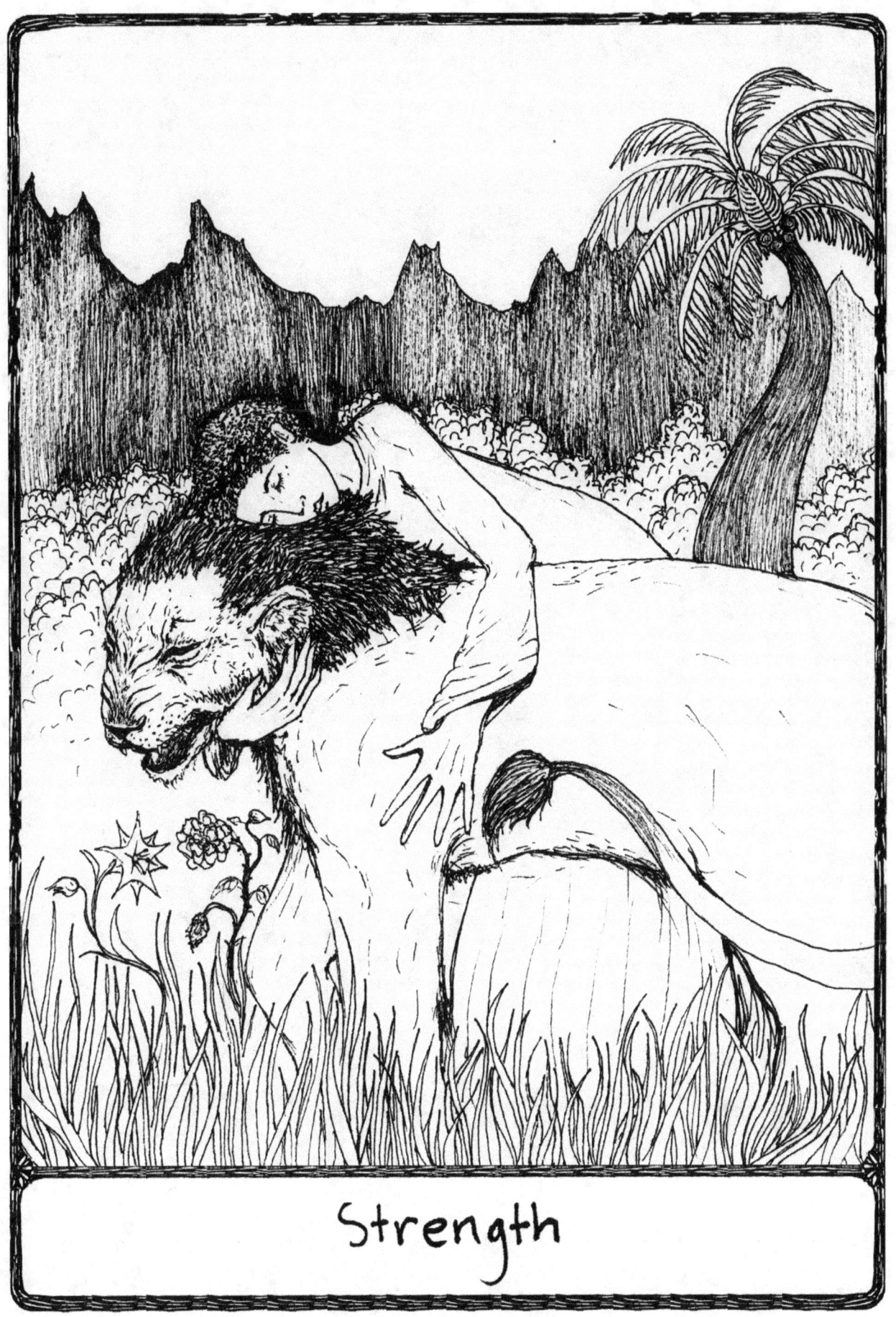

Strength

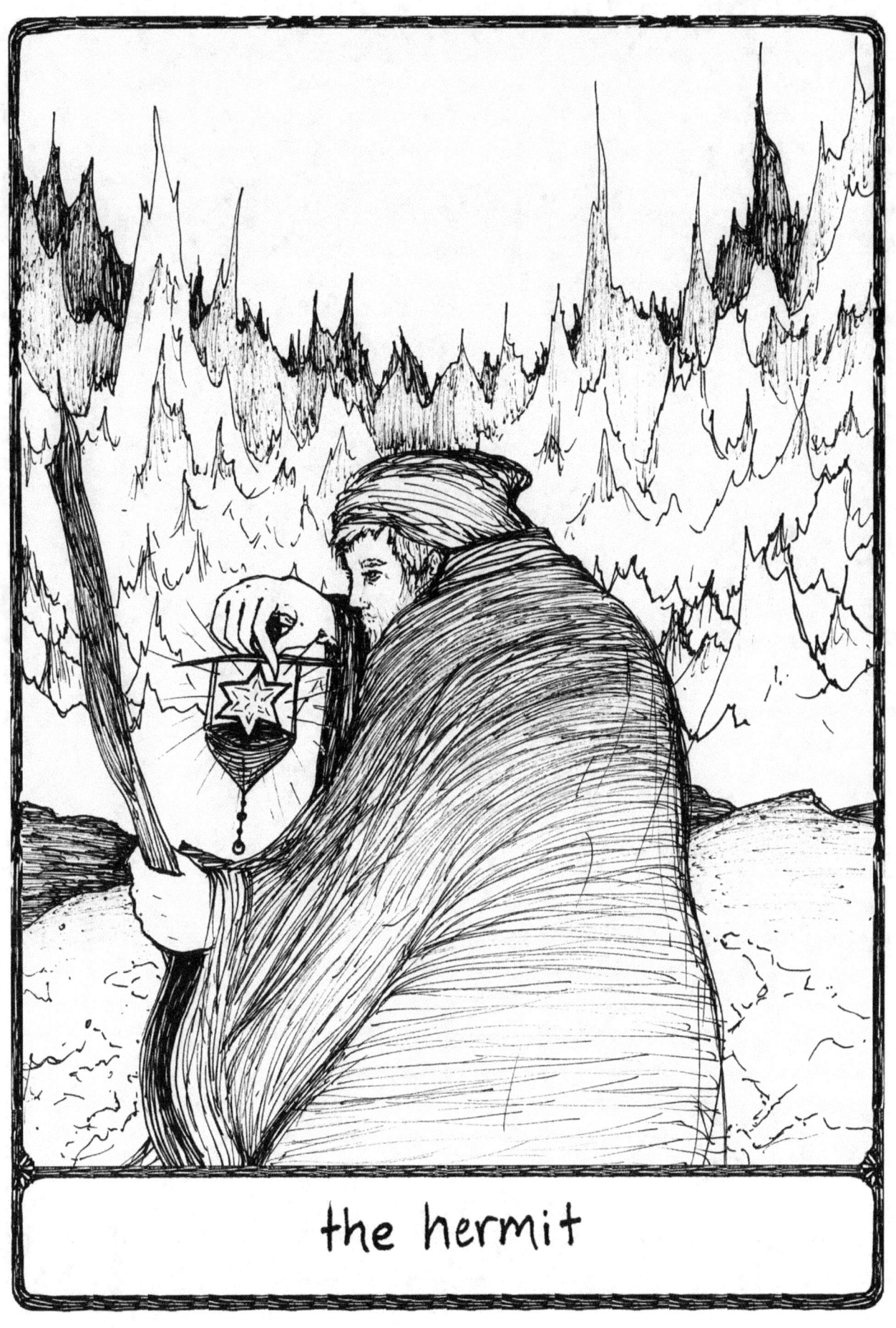

the hermit

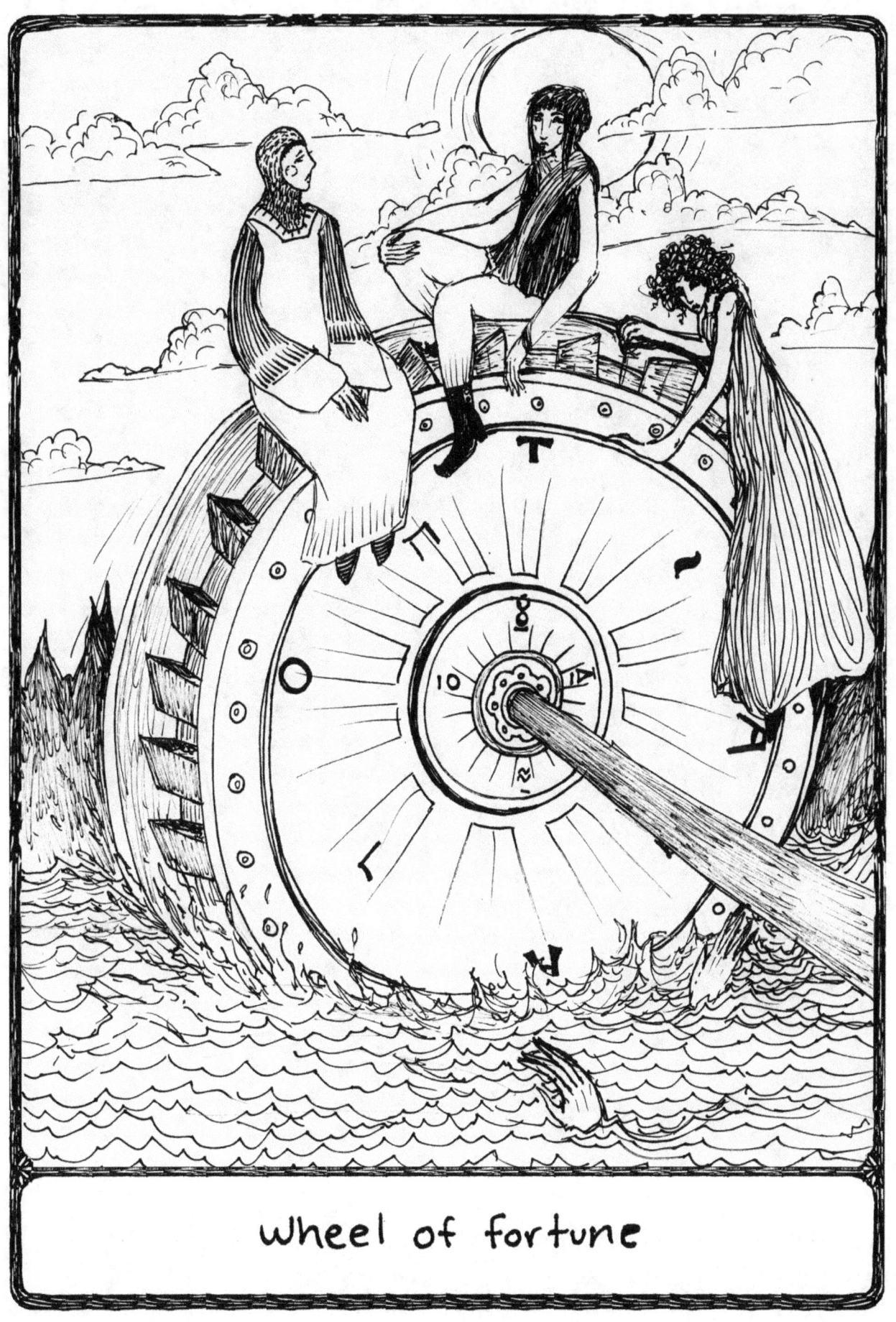

wheel of fortune

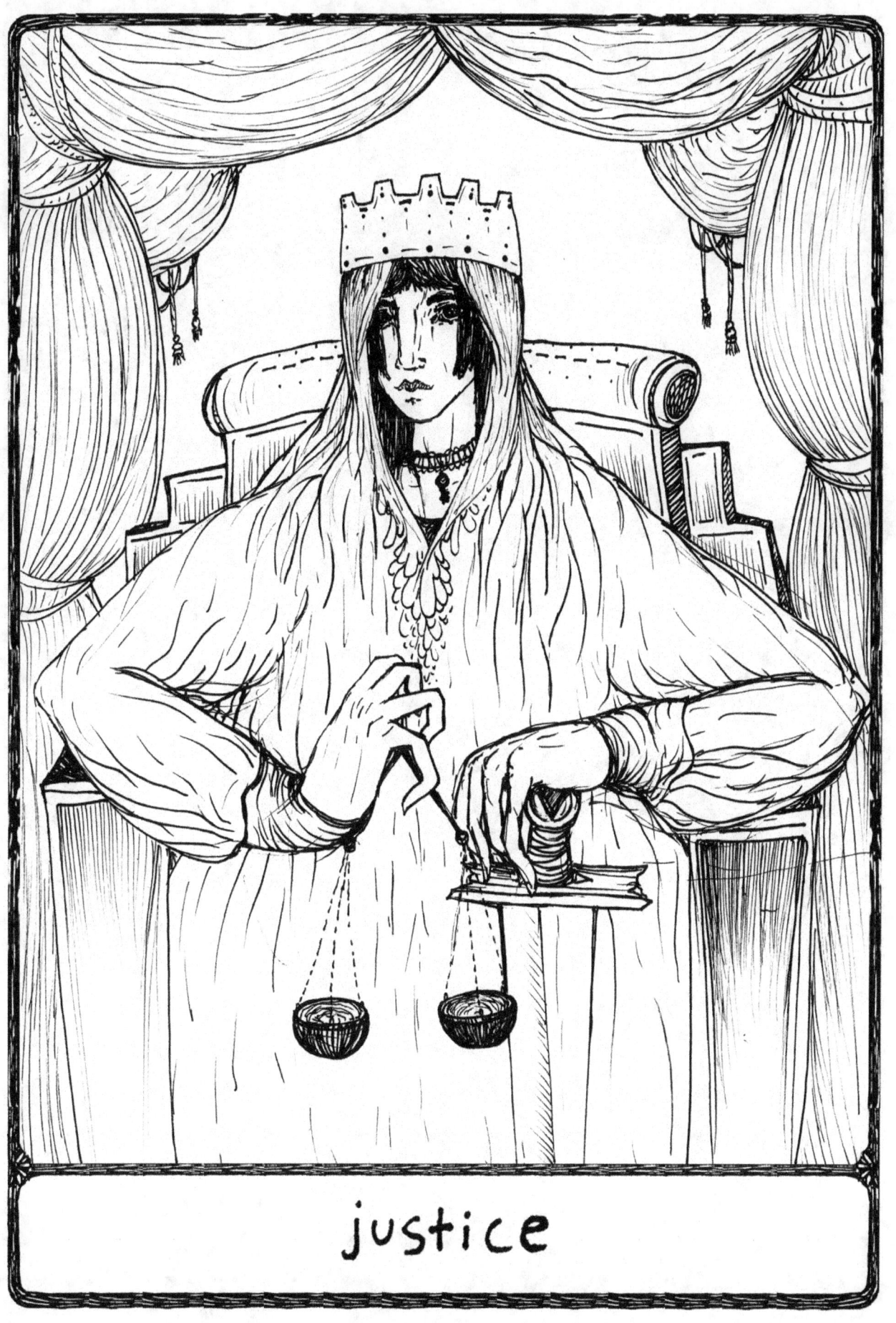

justice

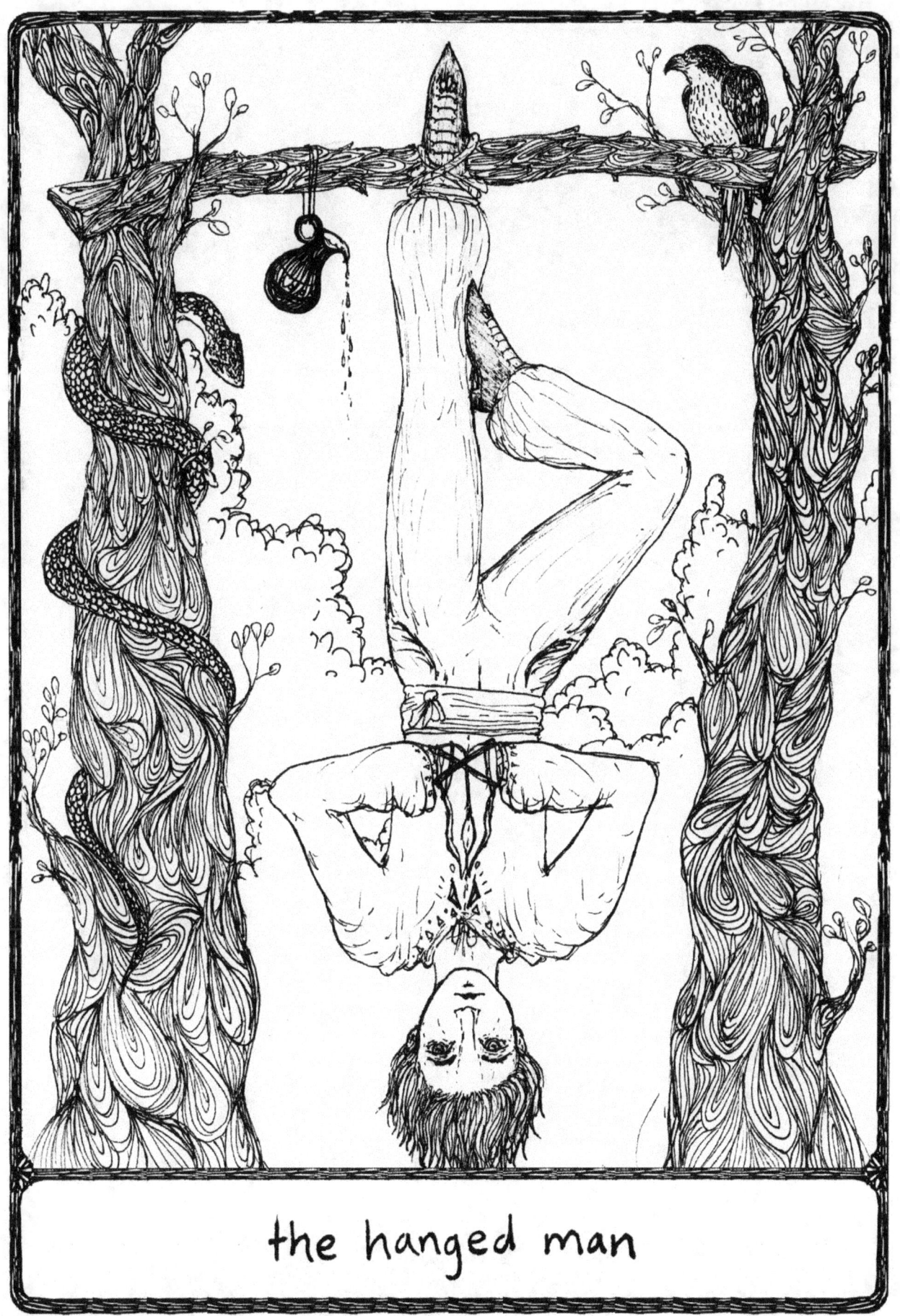

the hanged man

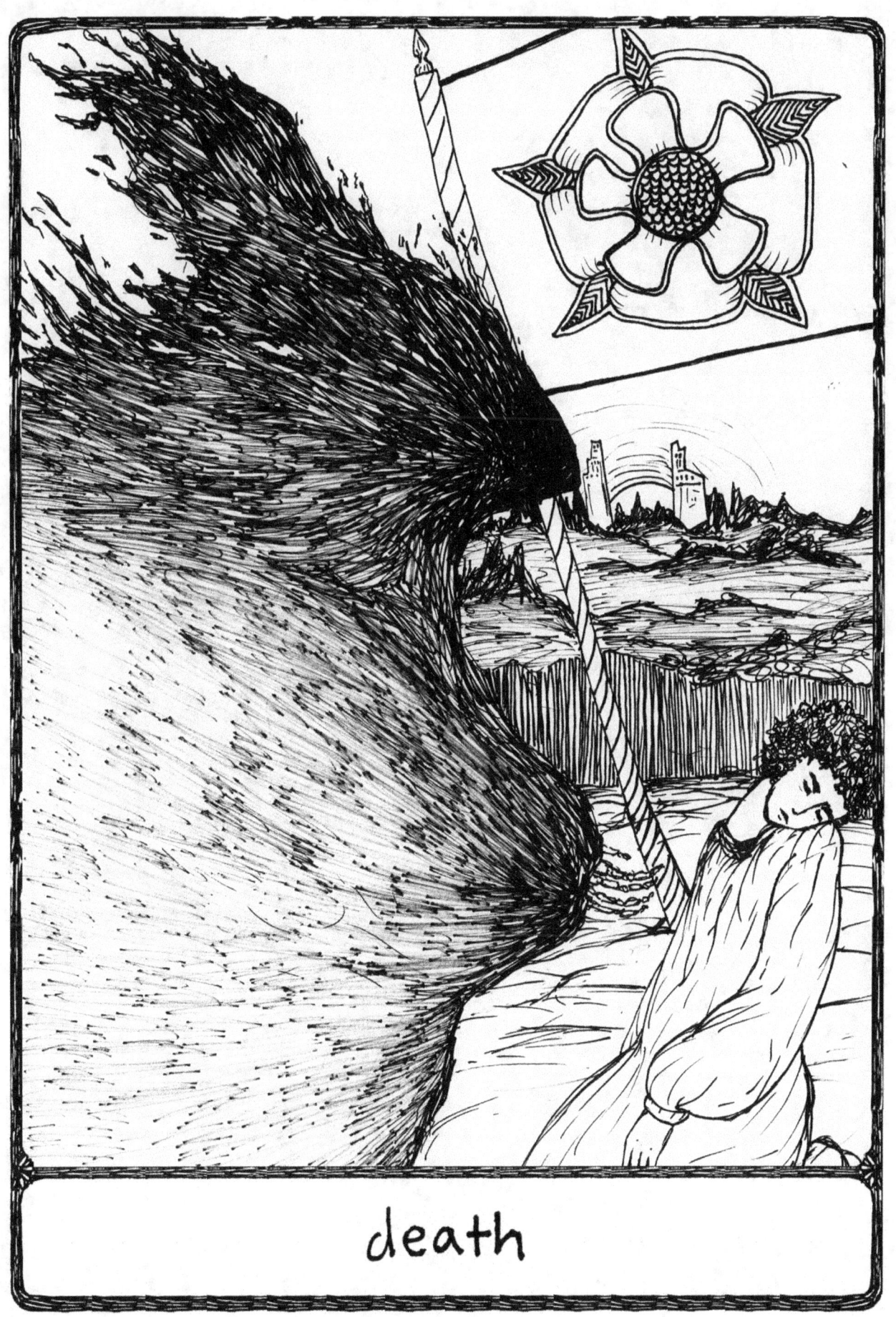

death

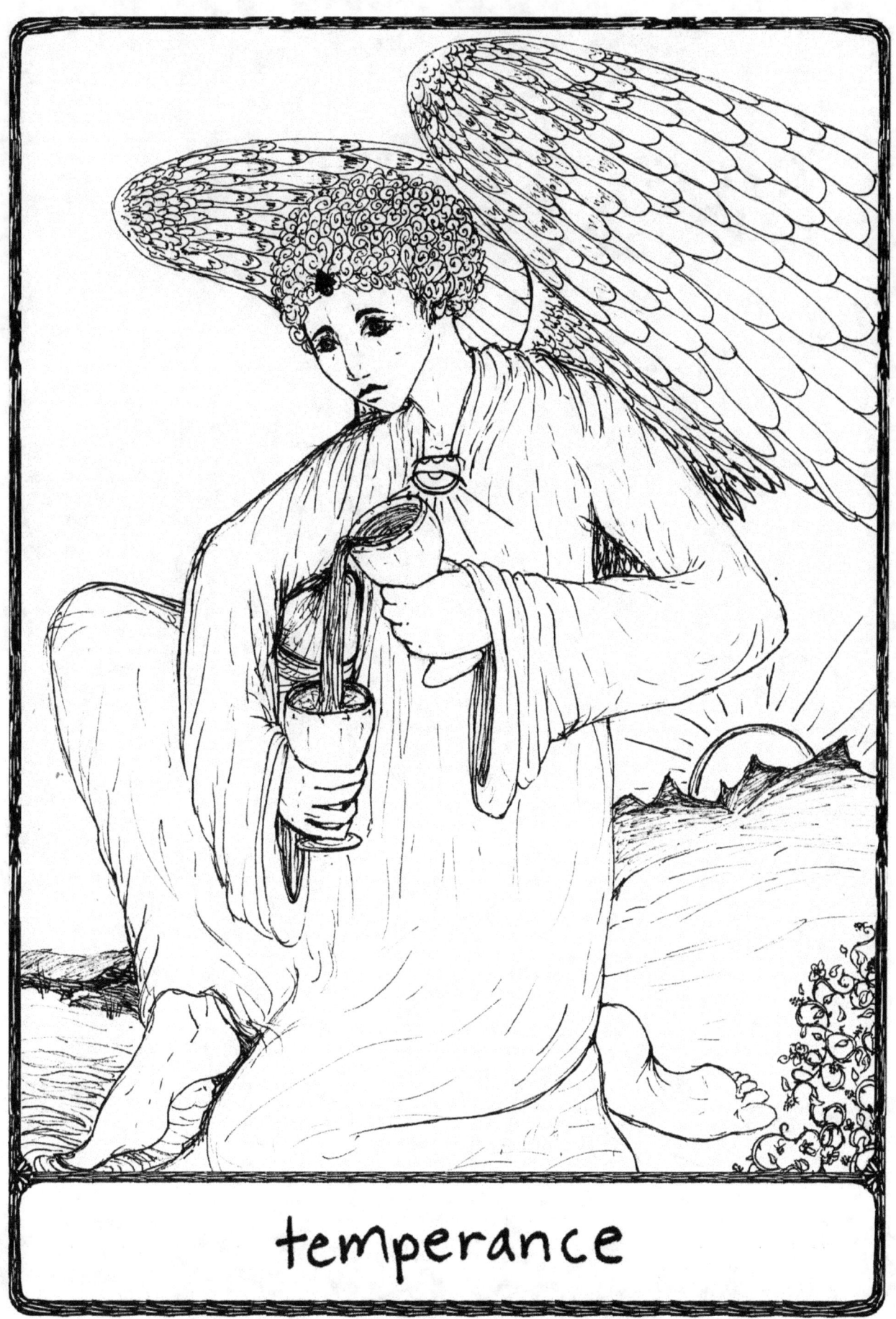

temperance

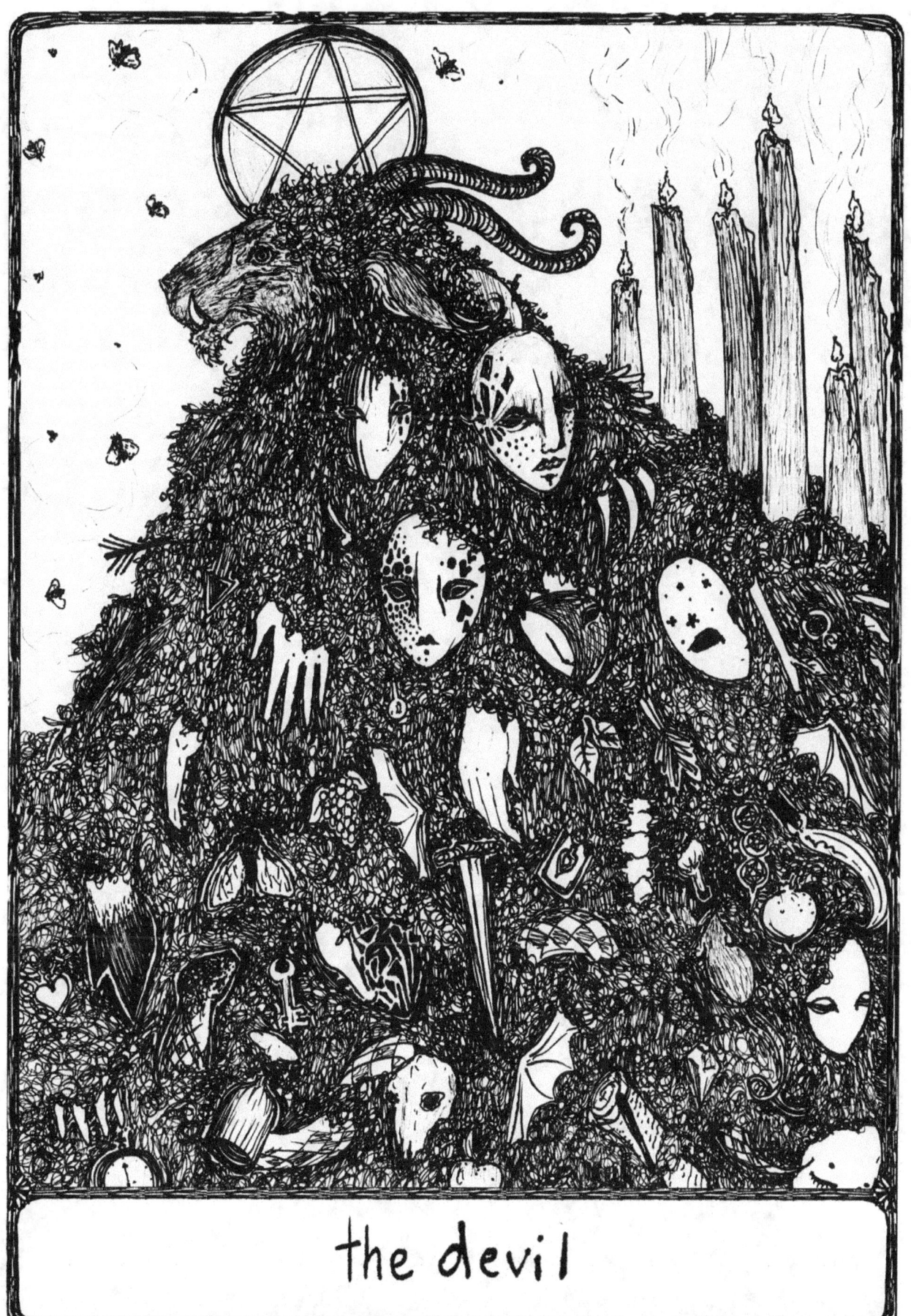

the devil

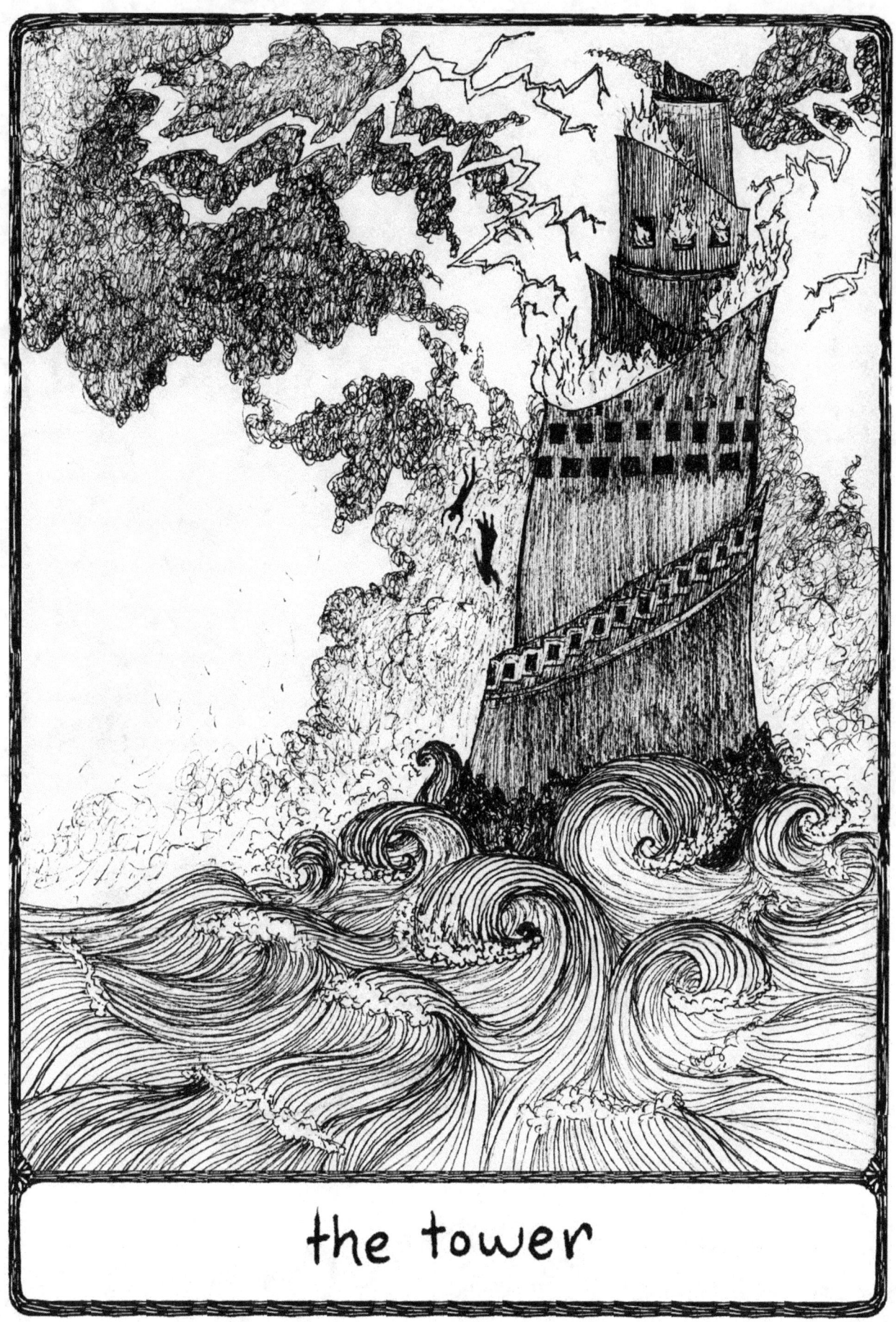

the tower

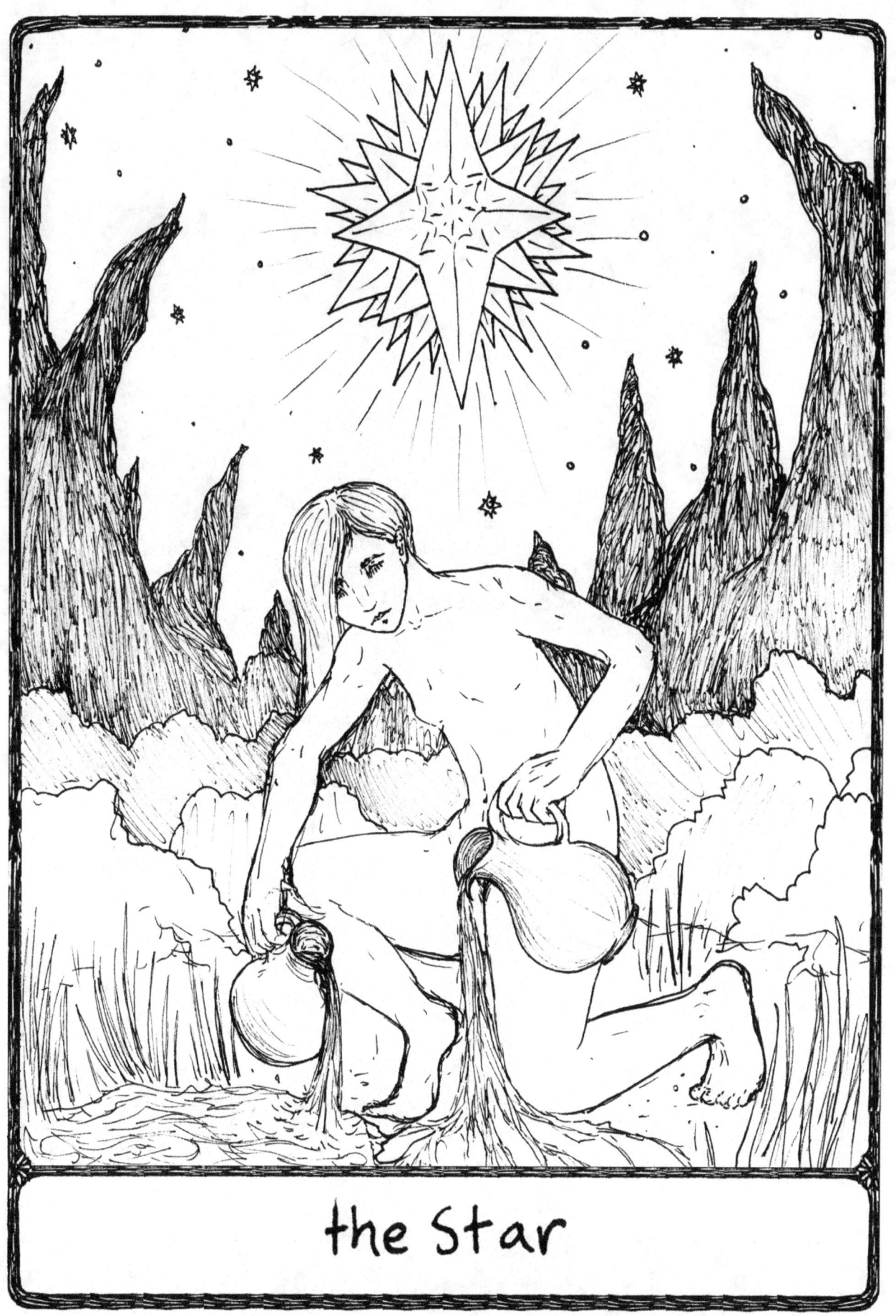

the Star

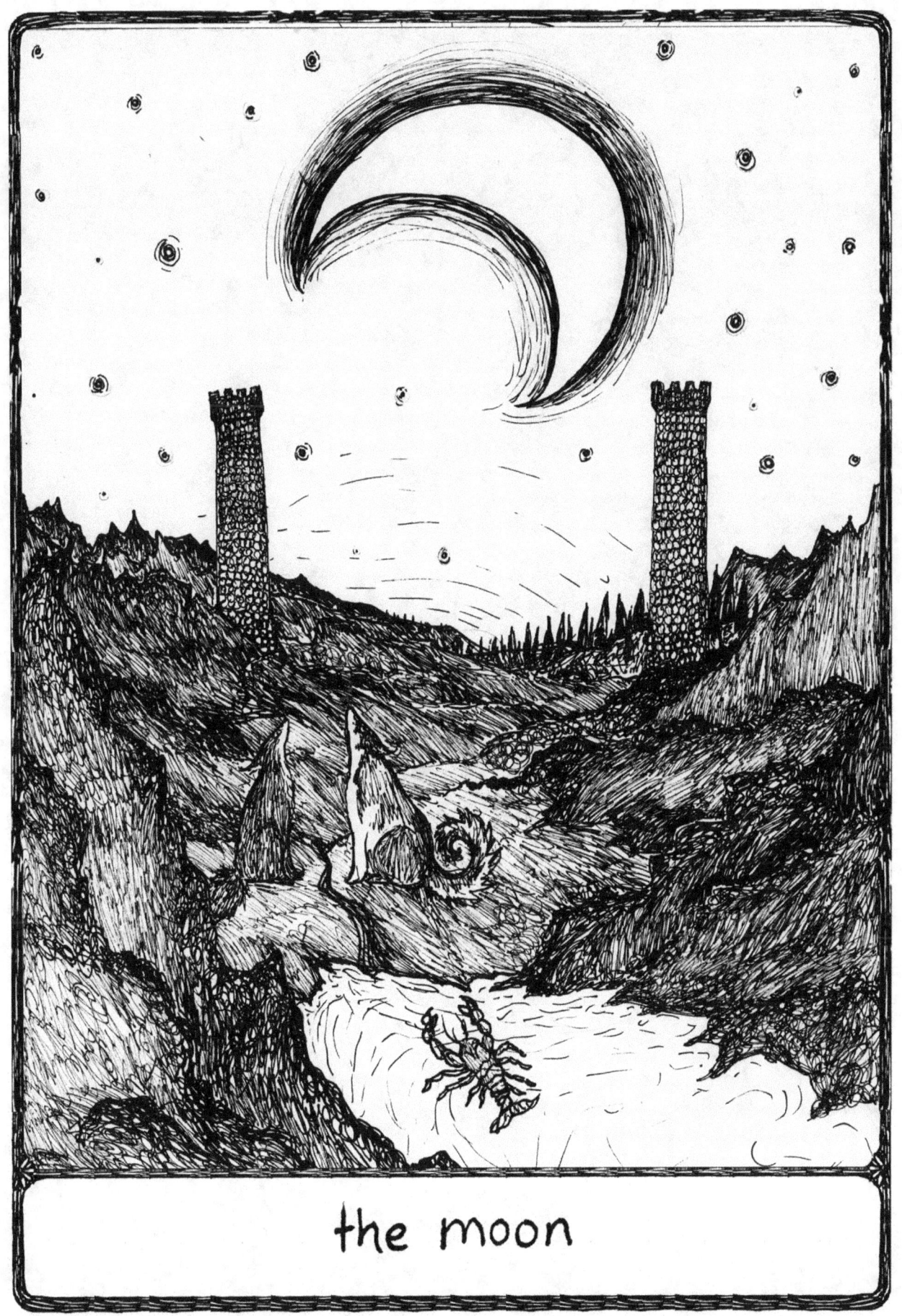

the moon

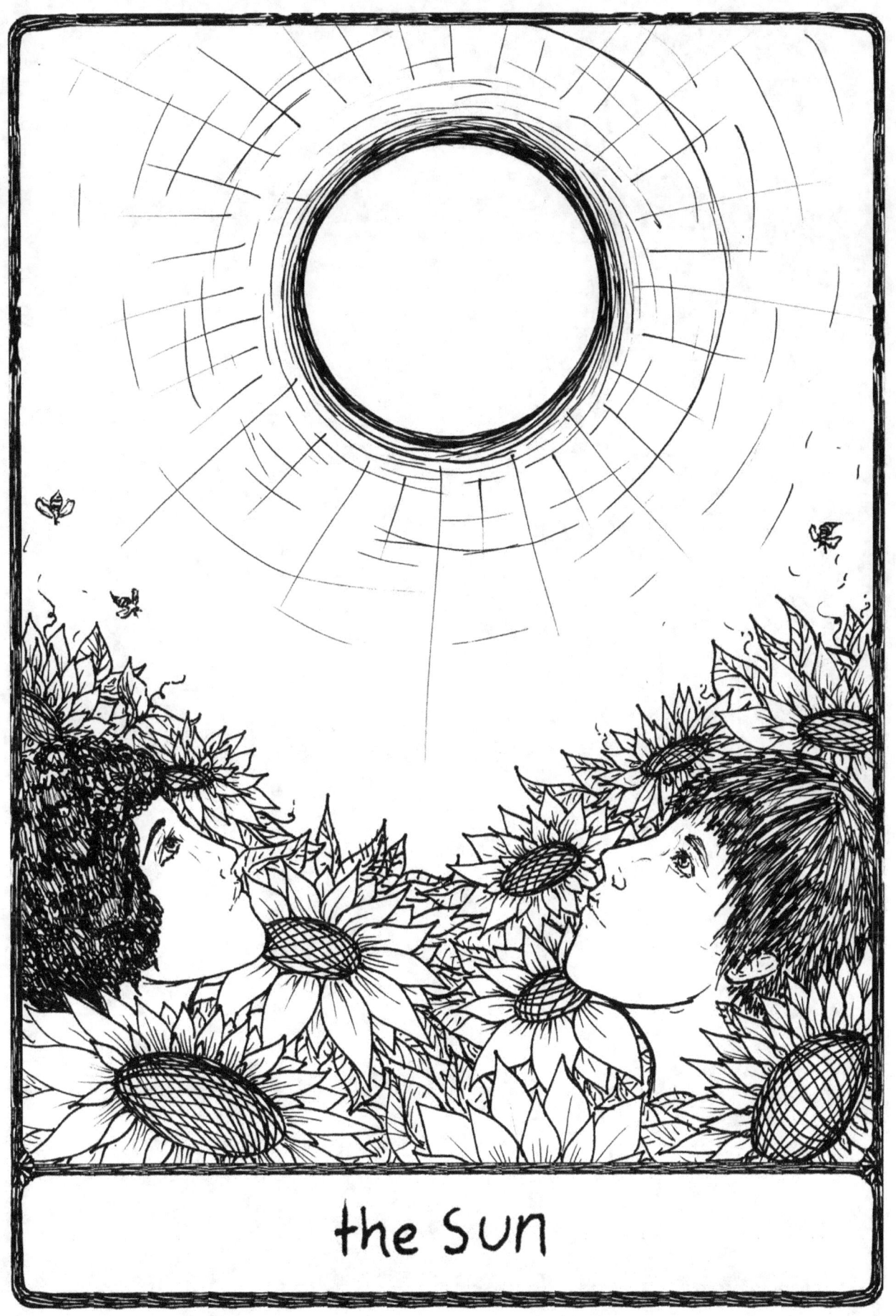

the sun

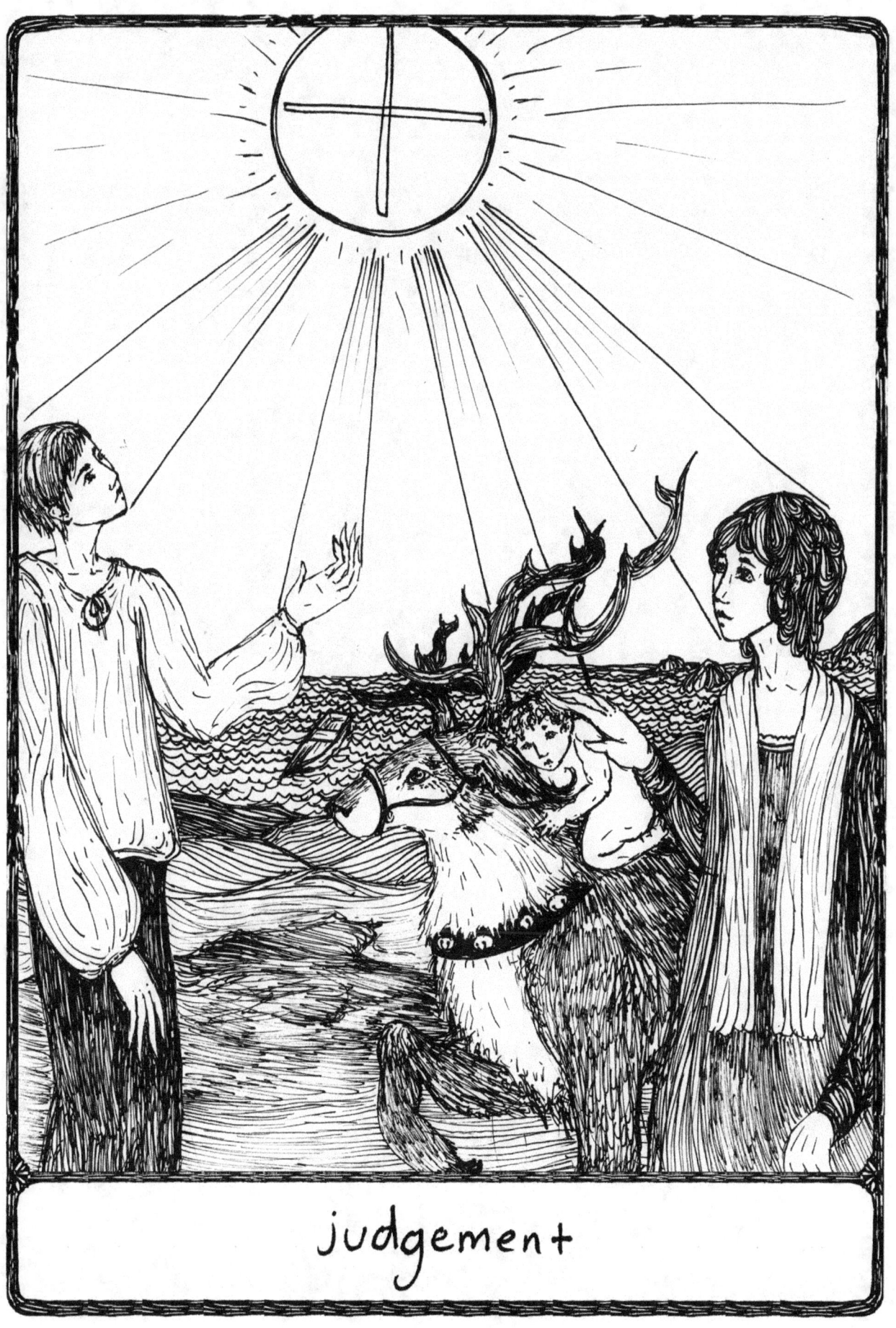

judgement

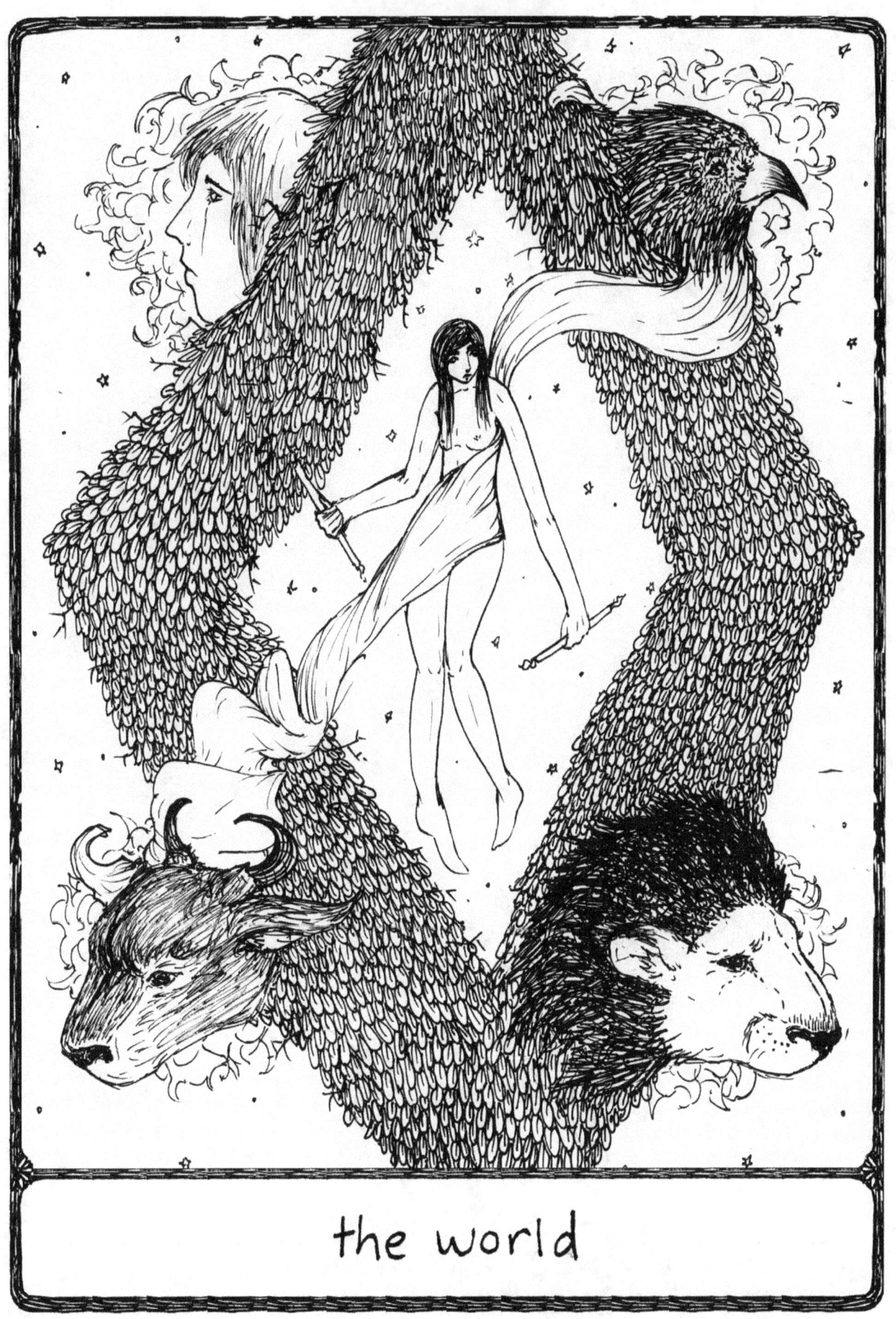

the world

the world

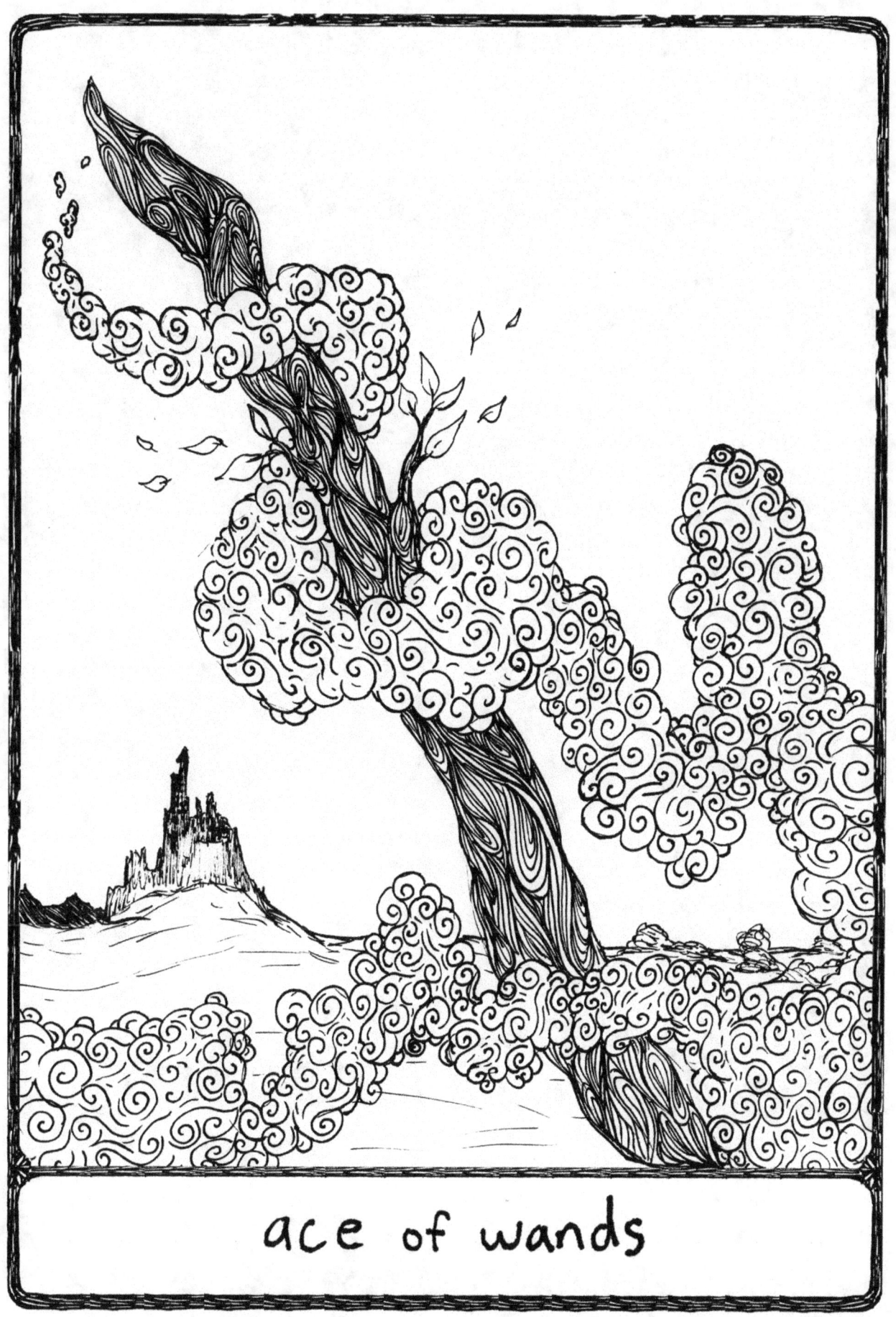

ace of wands

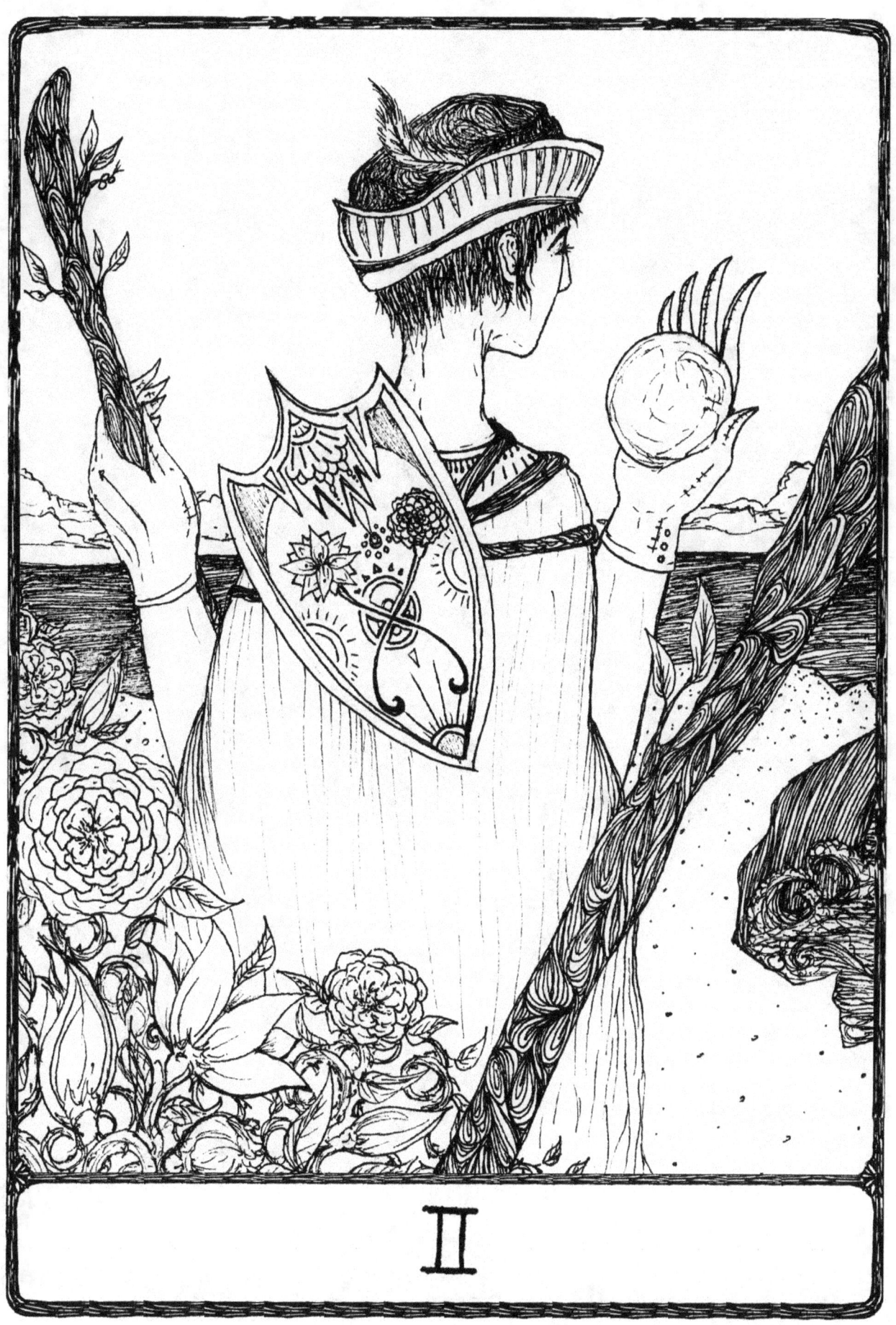

Ⅱ

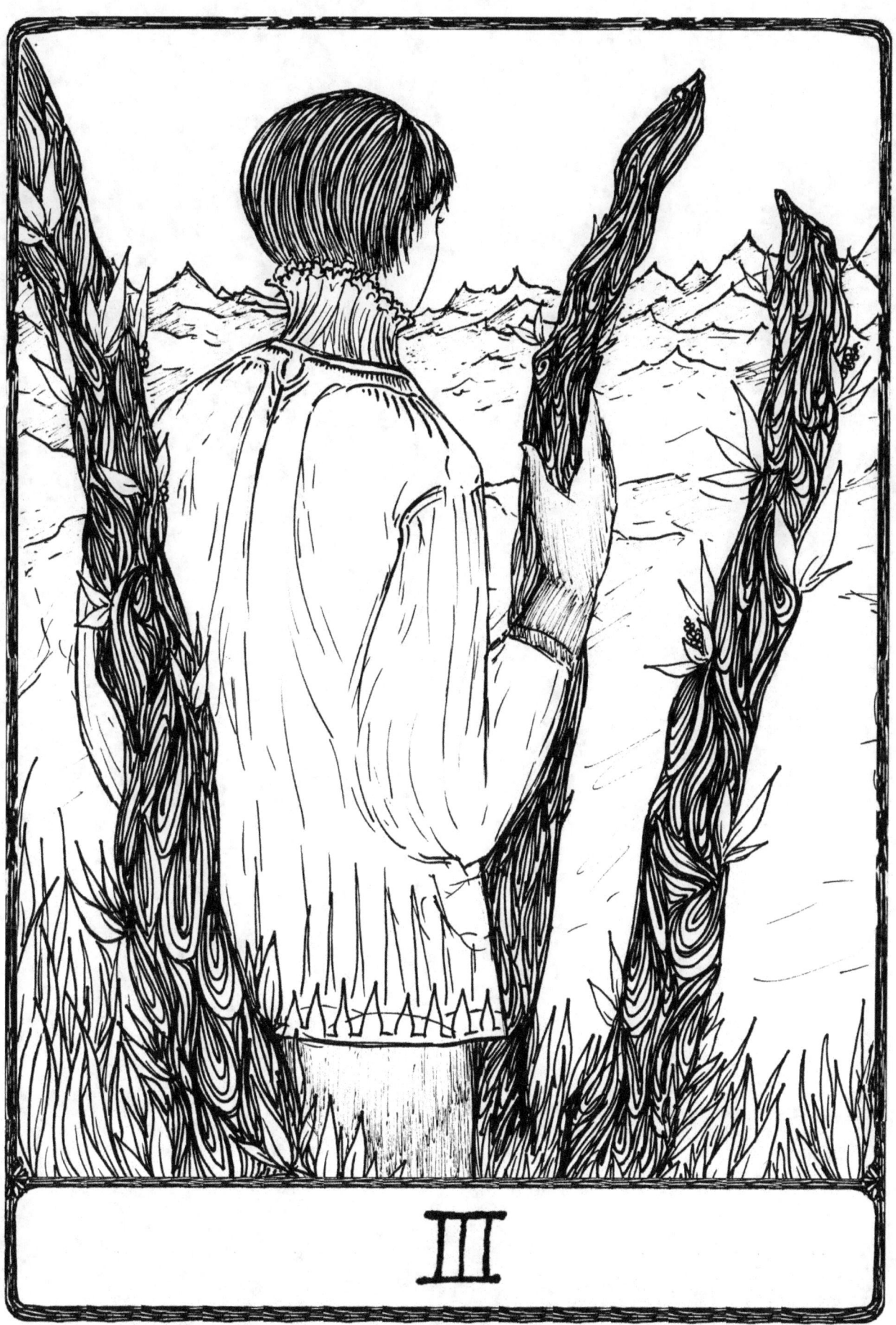

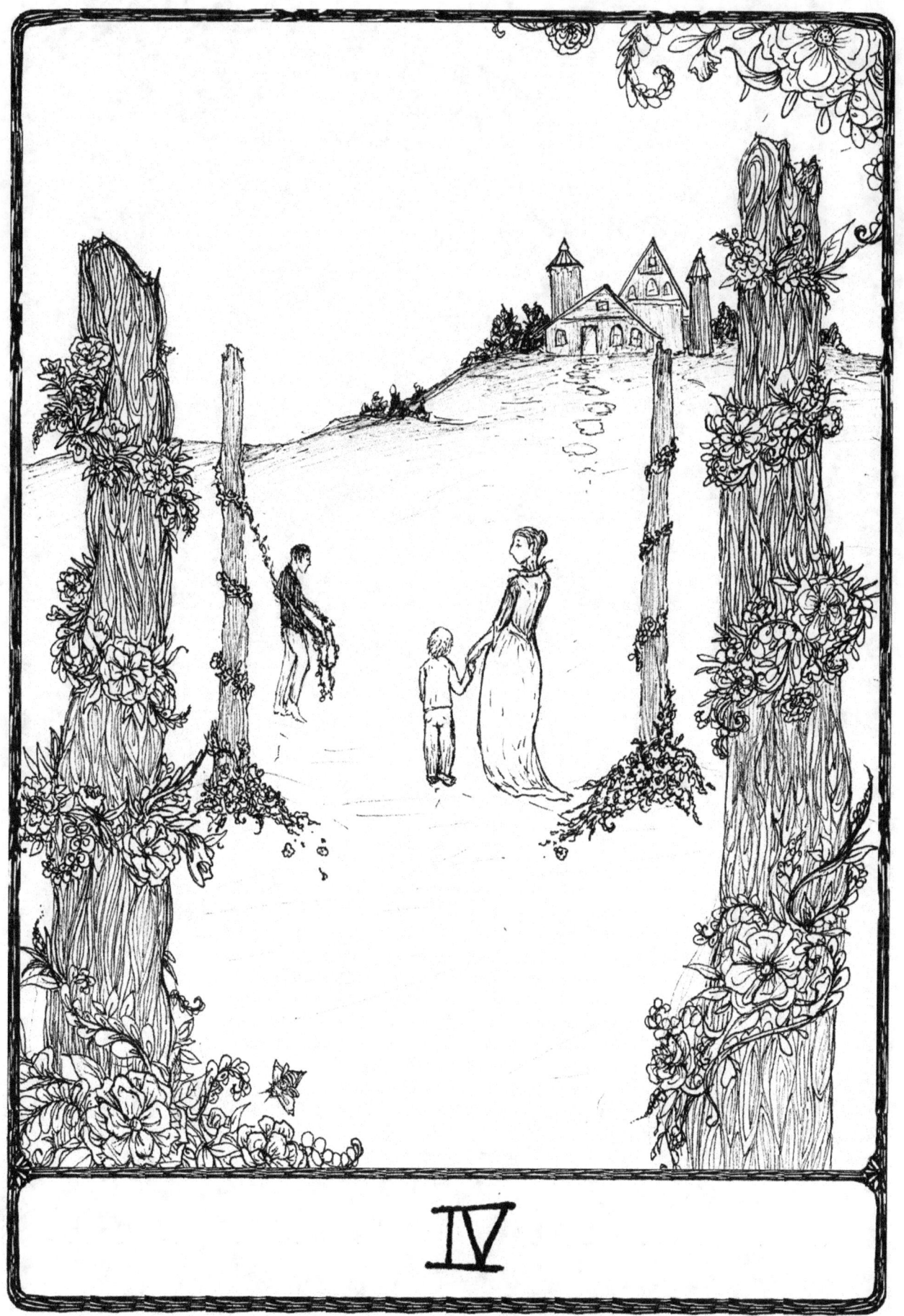

IV

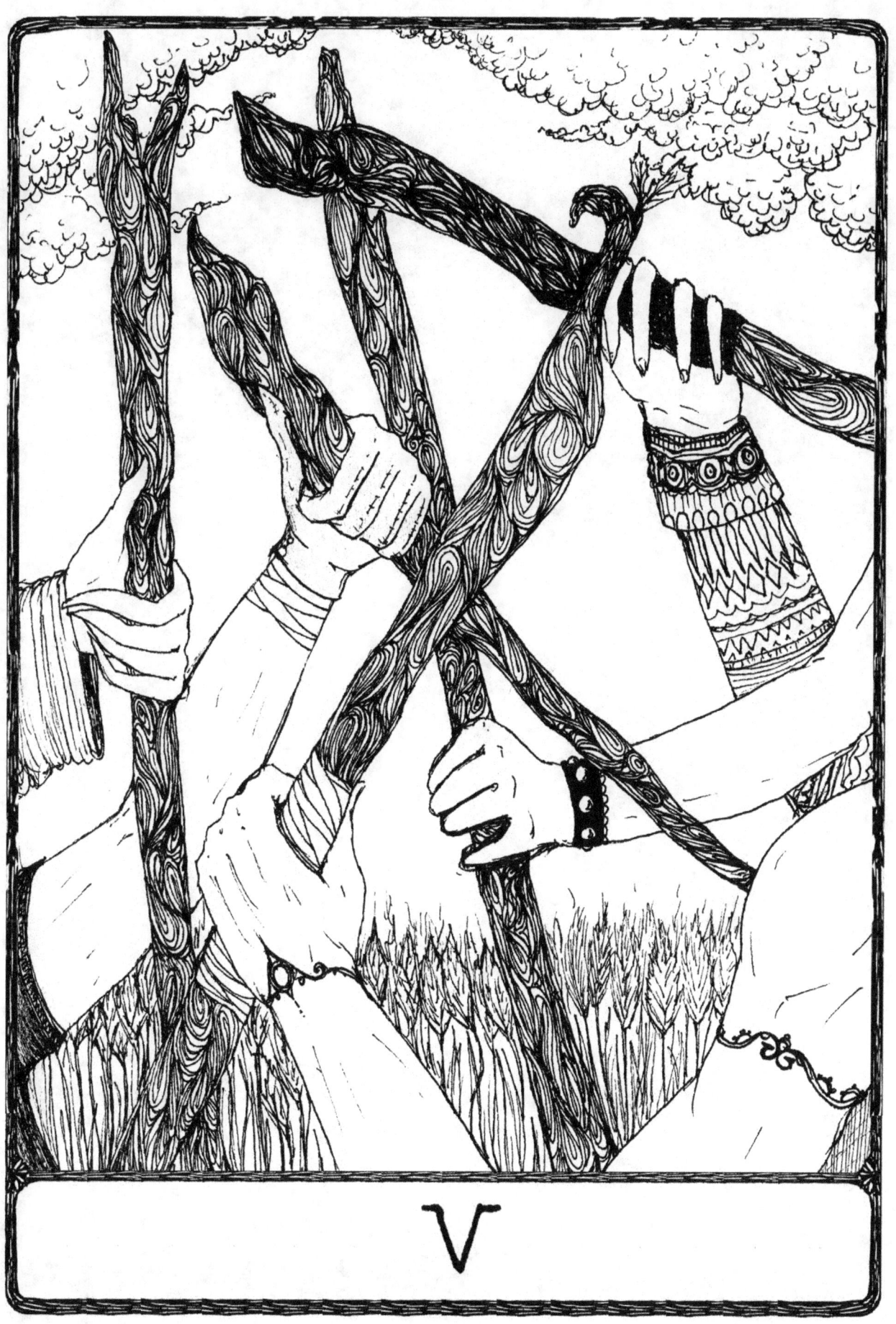

V

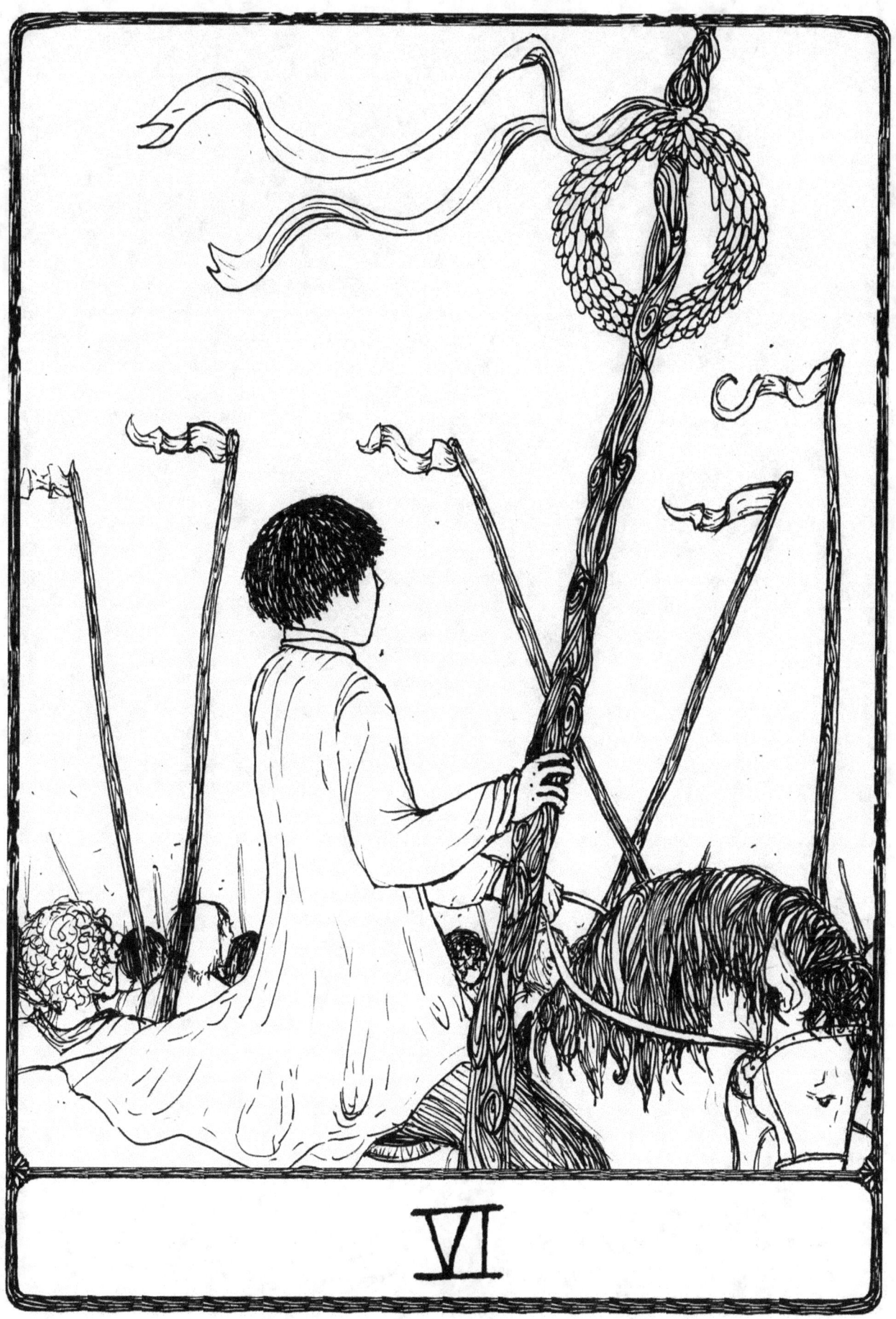

VI

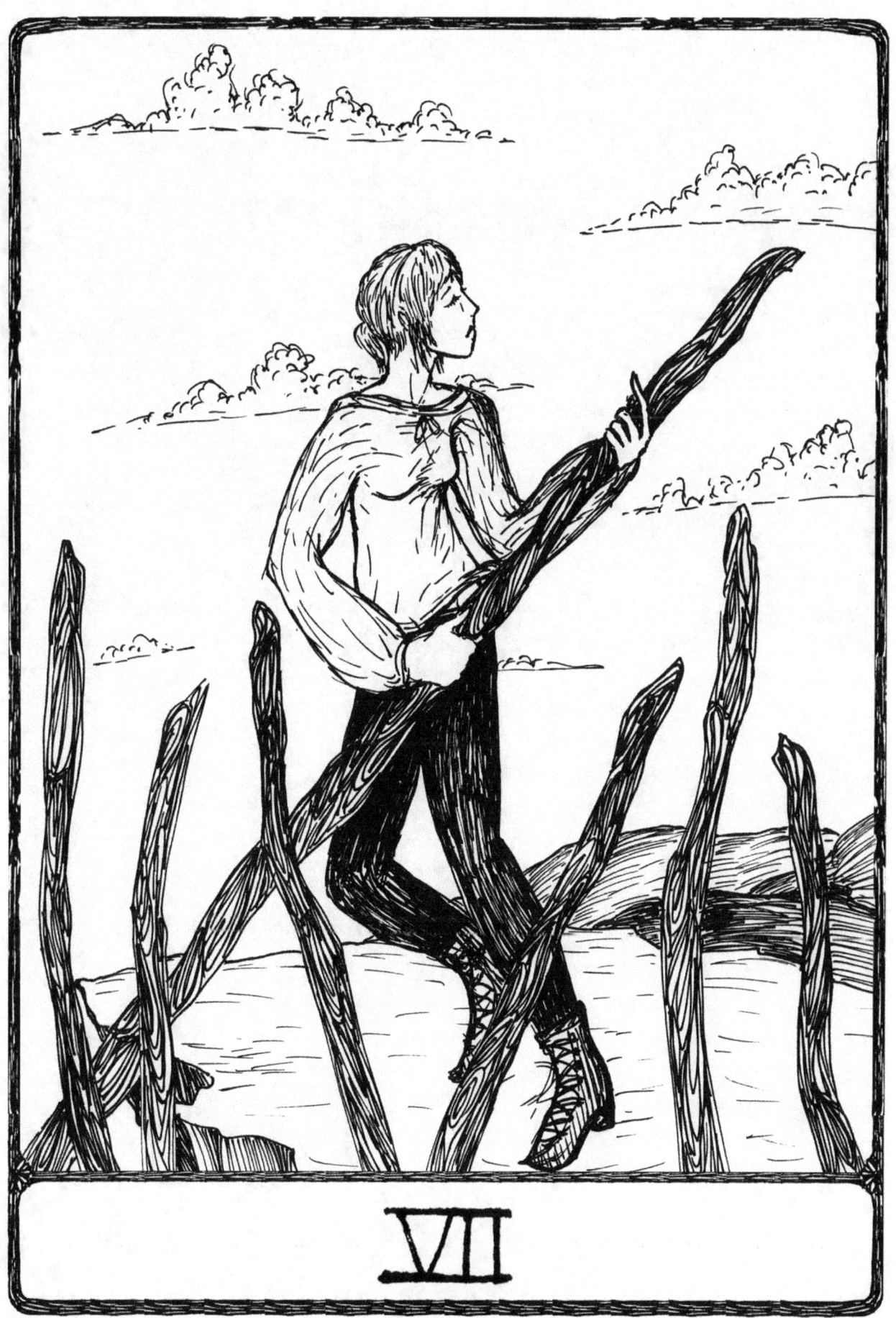

VII

IV

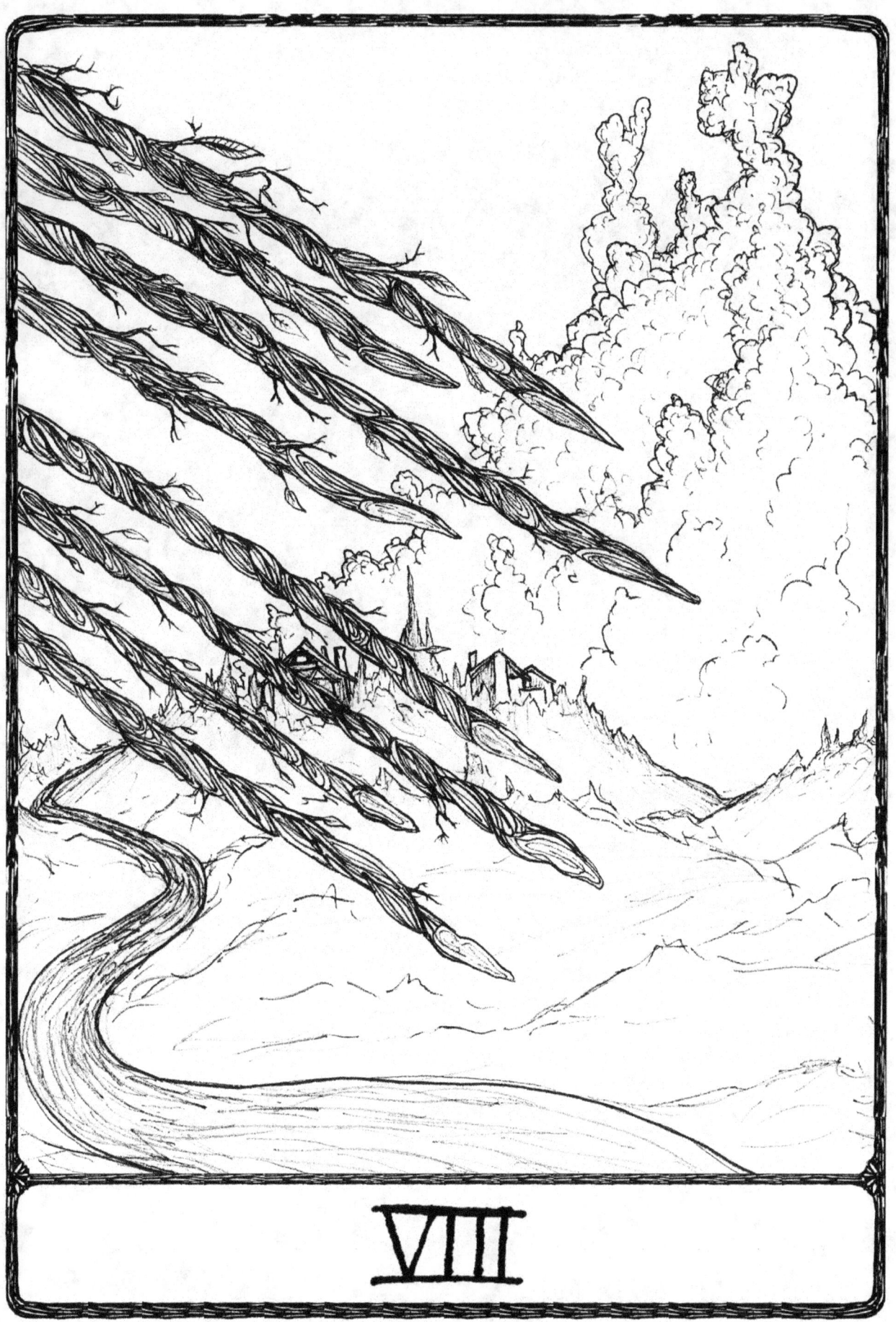

VIII

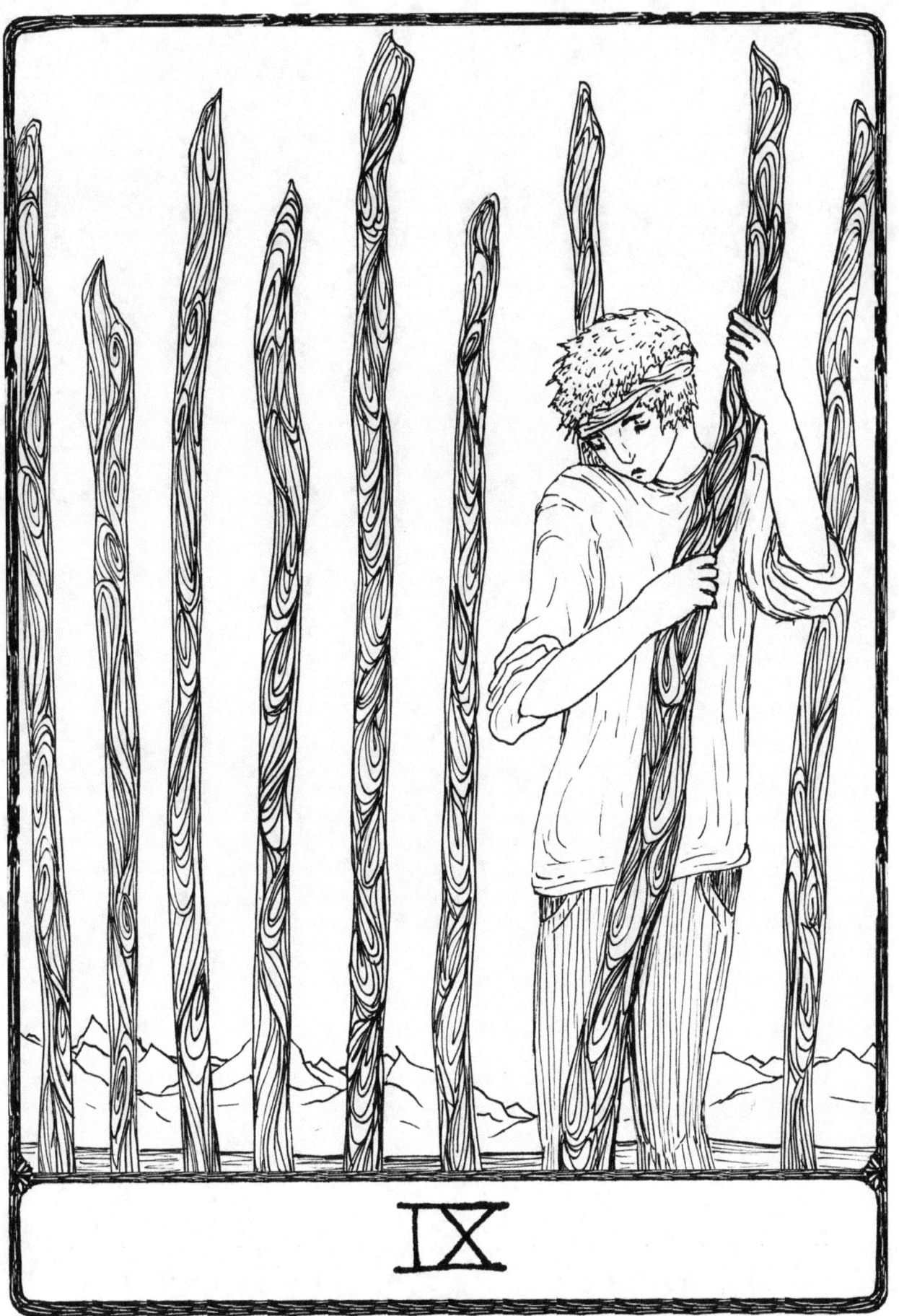

IX

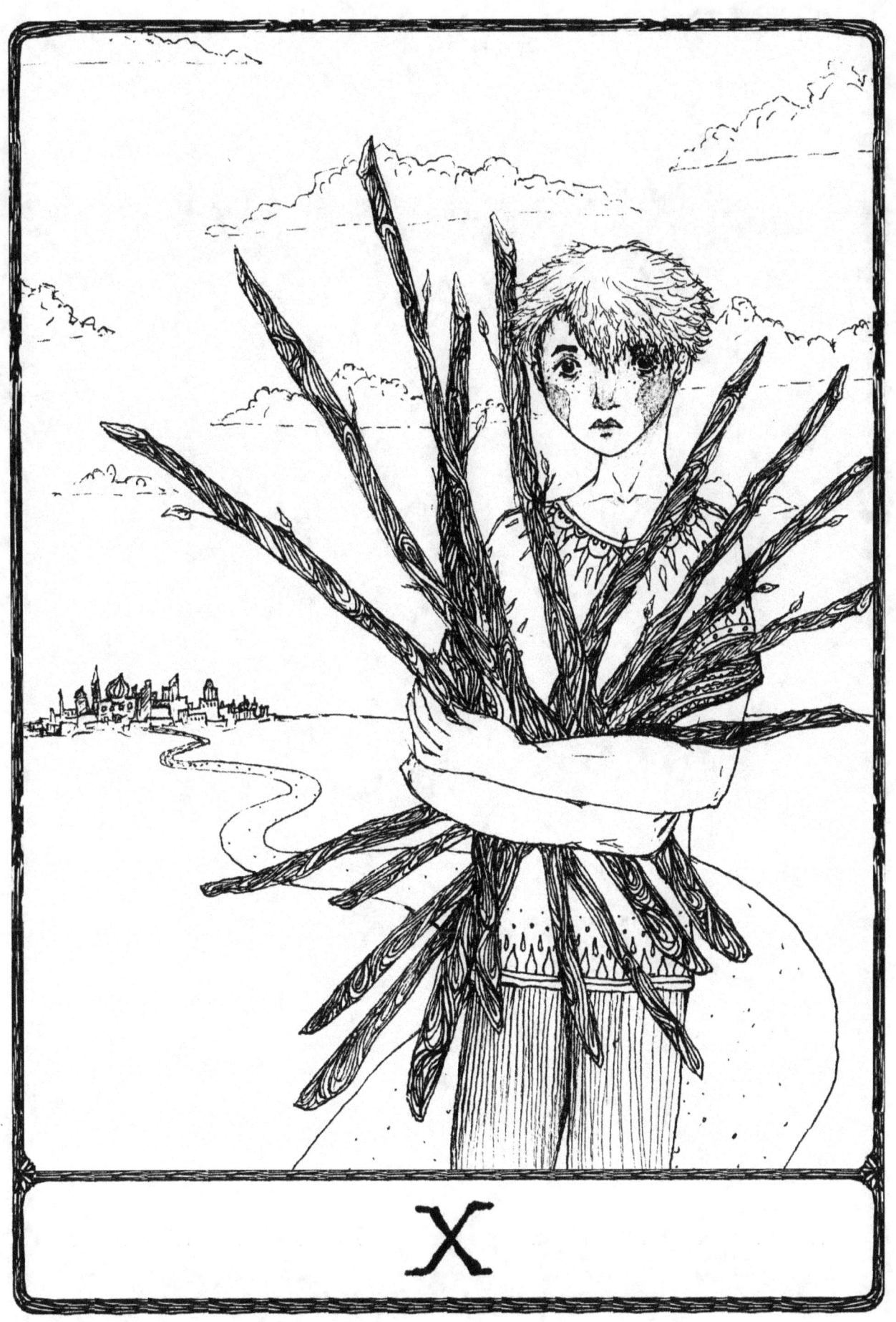

X

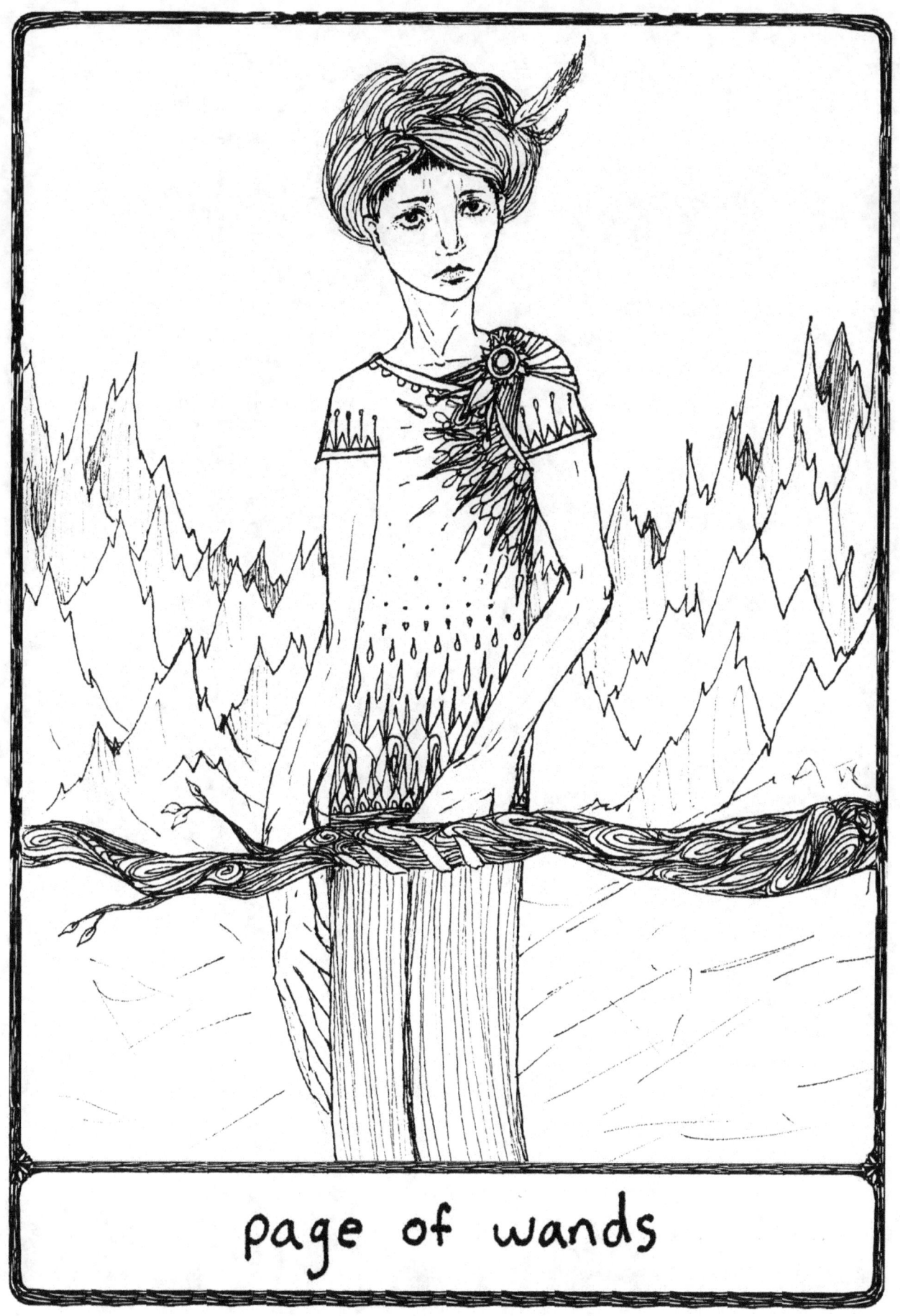

page of wands

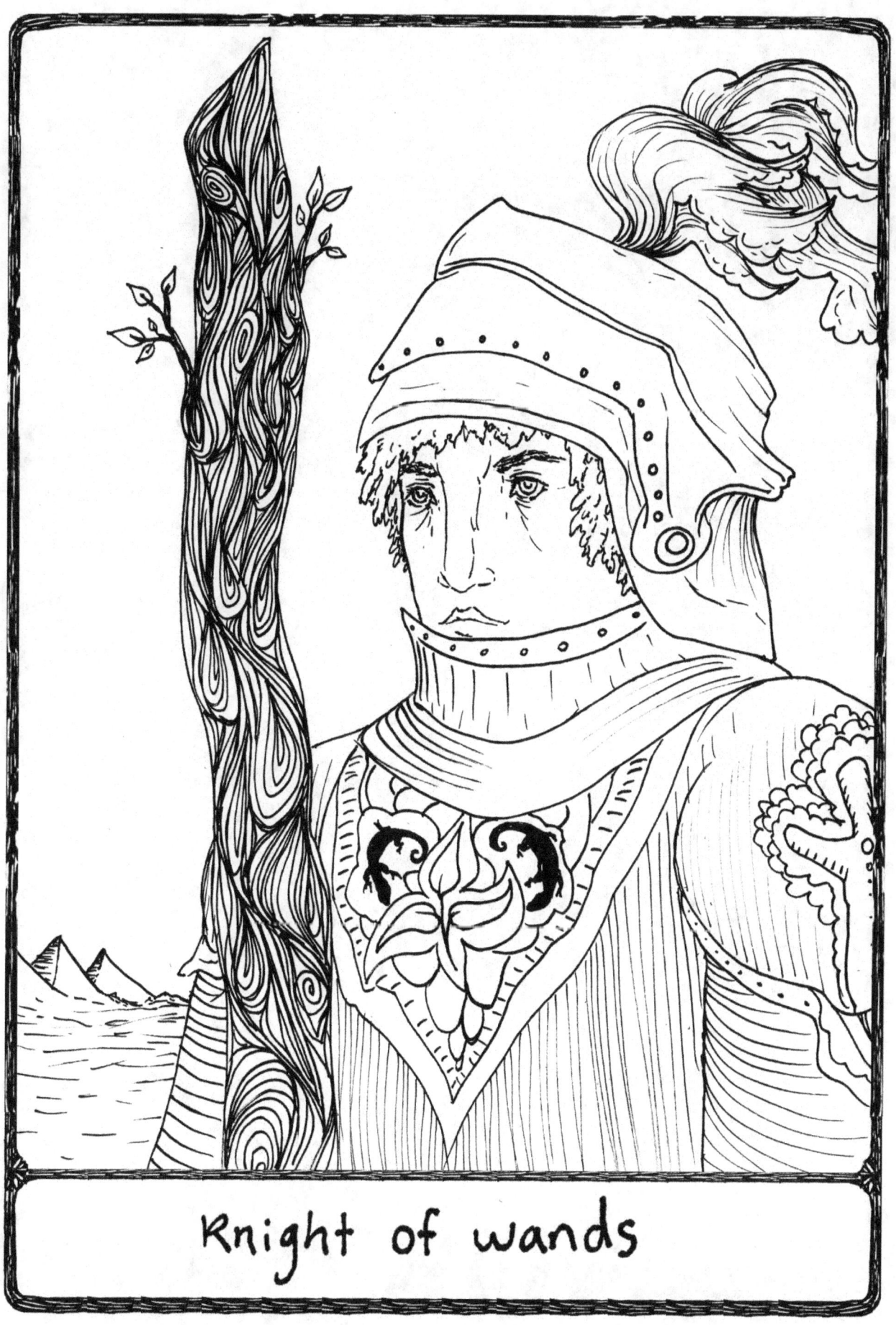

Knight of wands

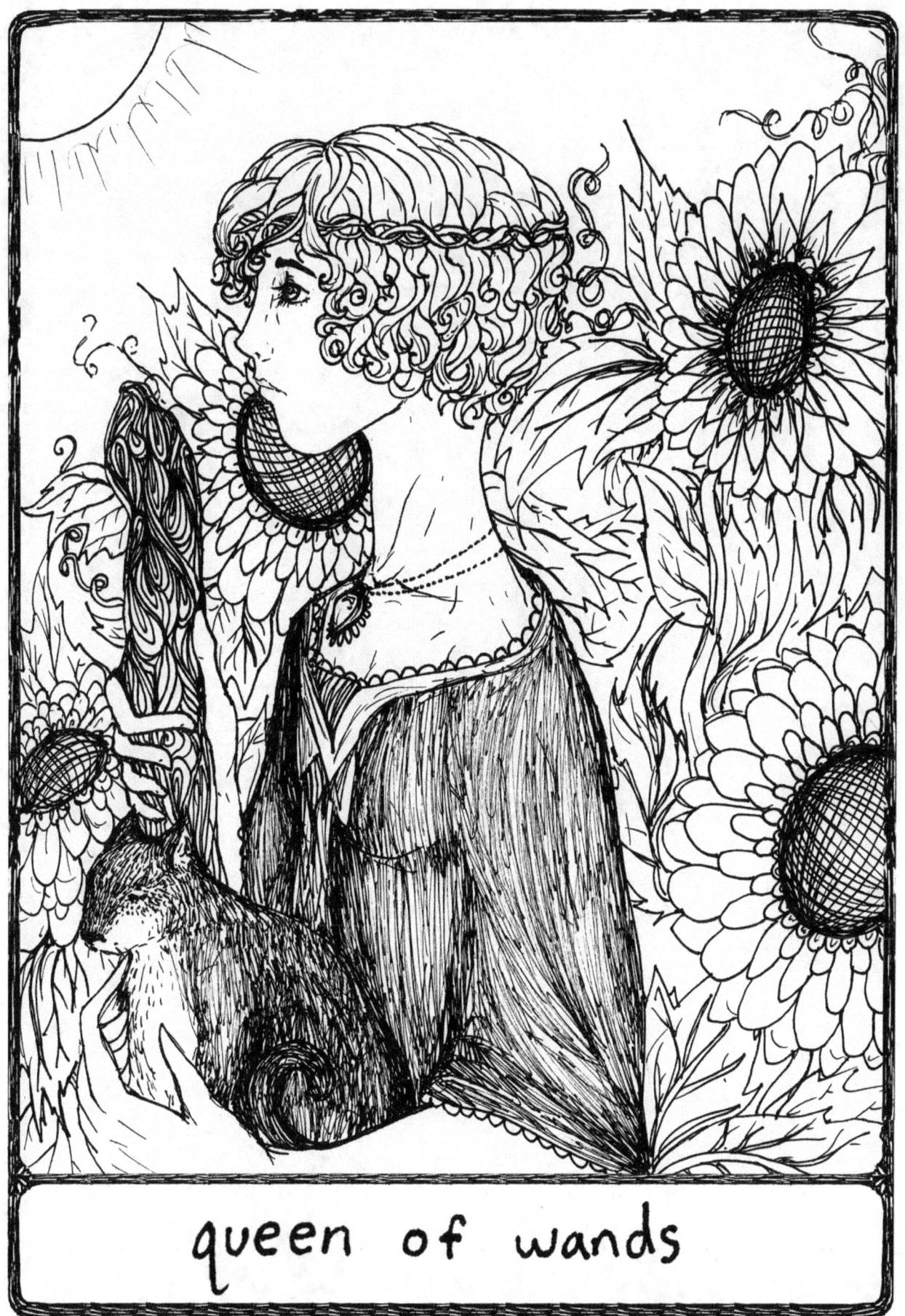

queen of wands

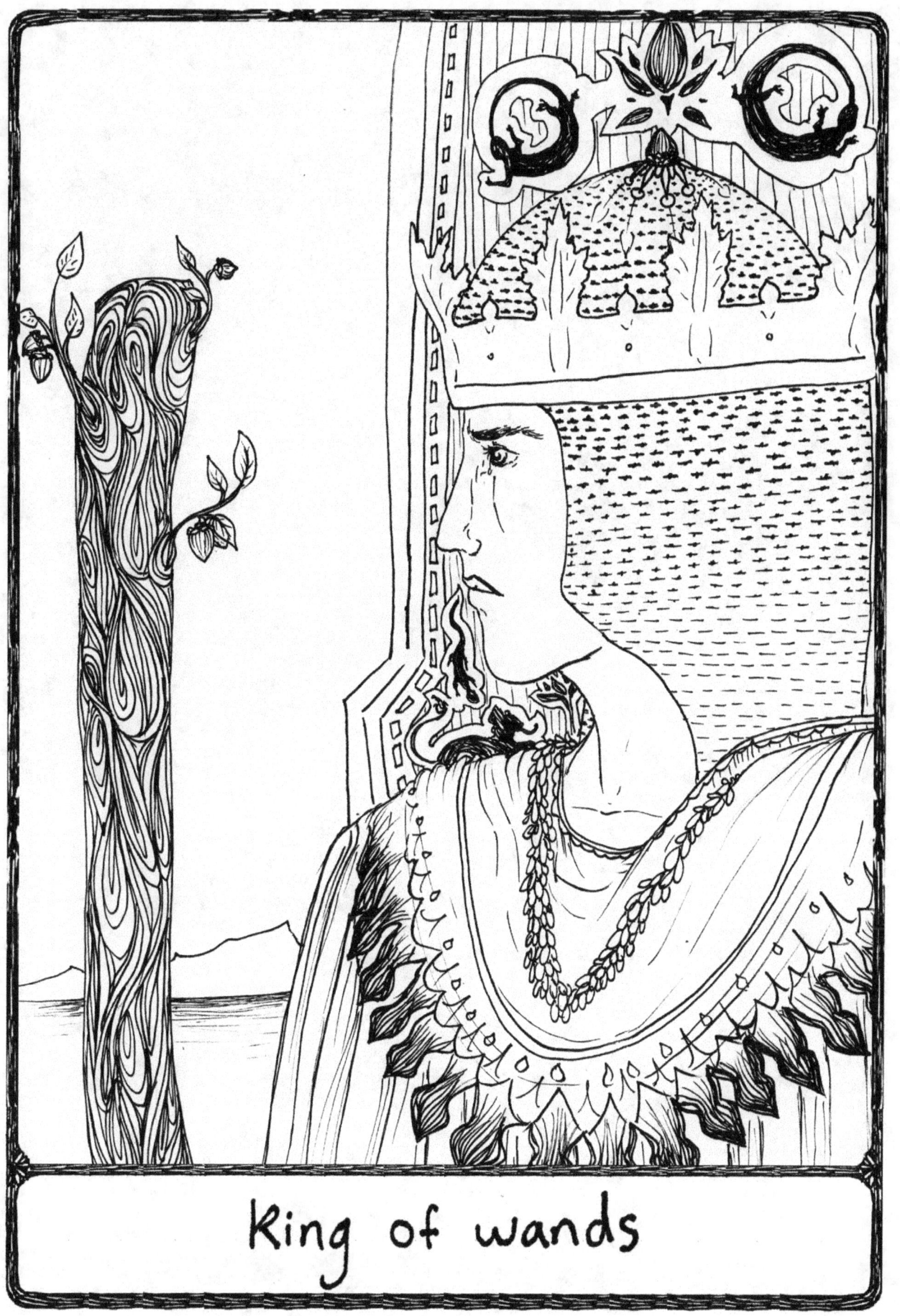

King of wands

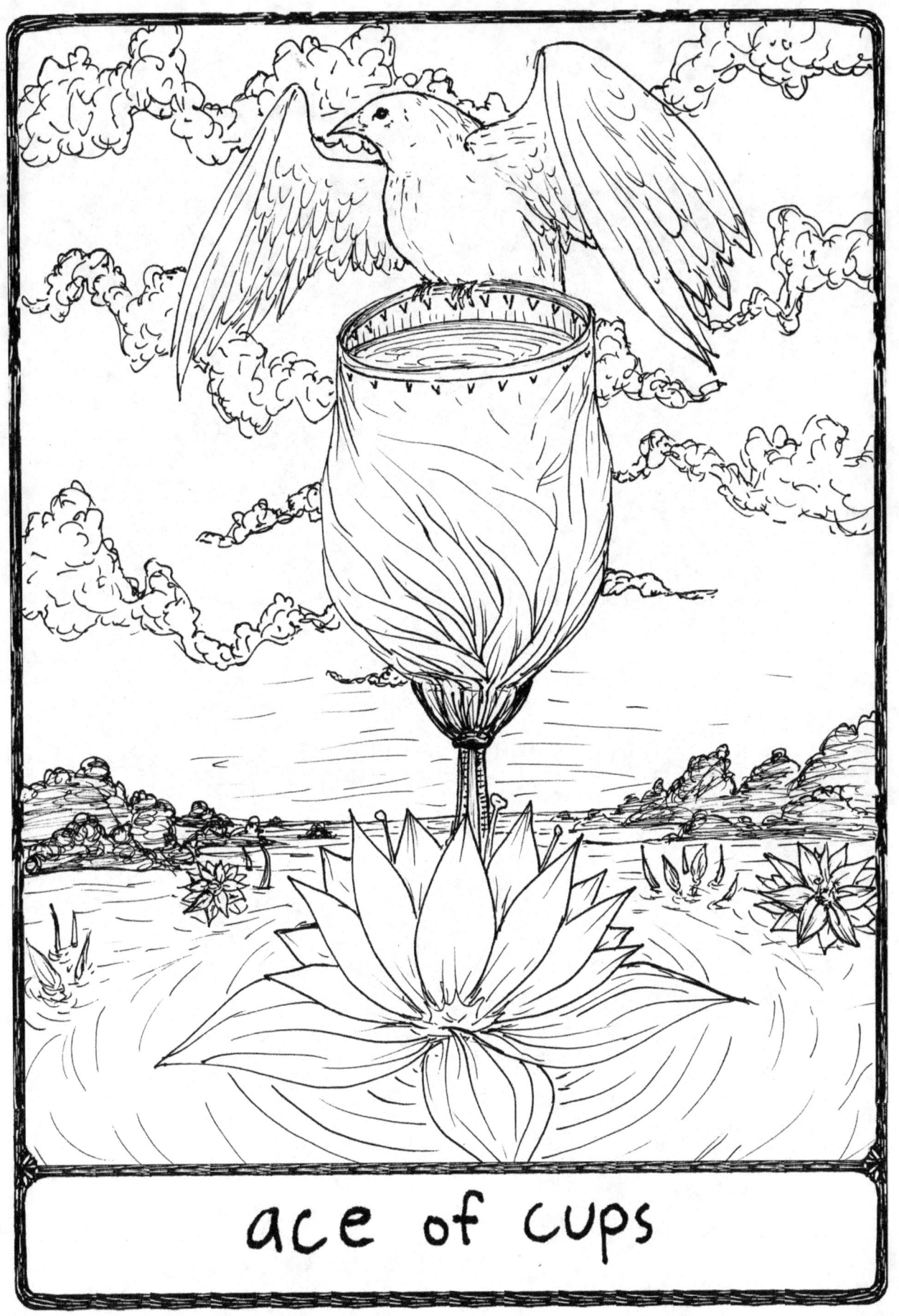

ace of cups

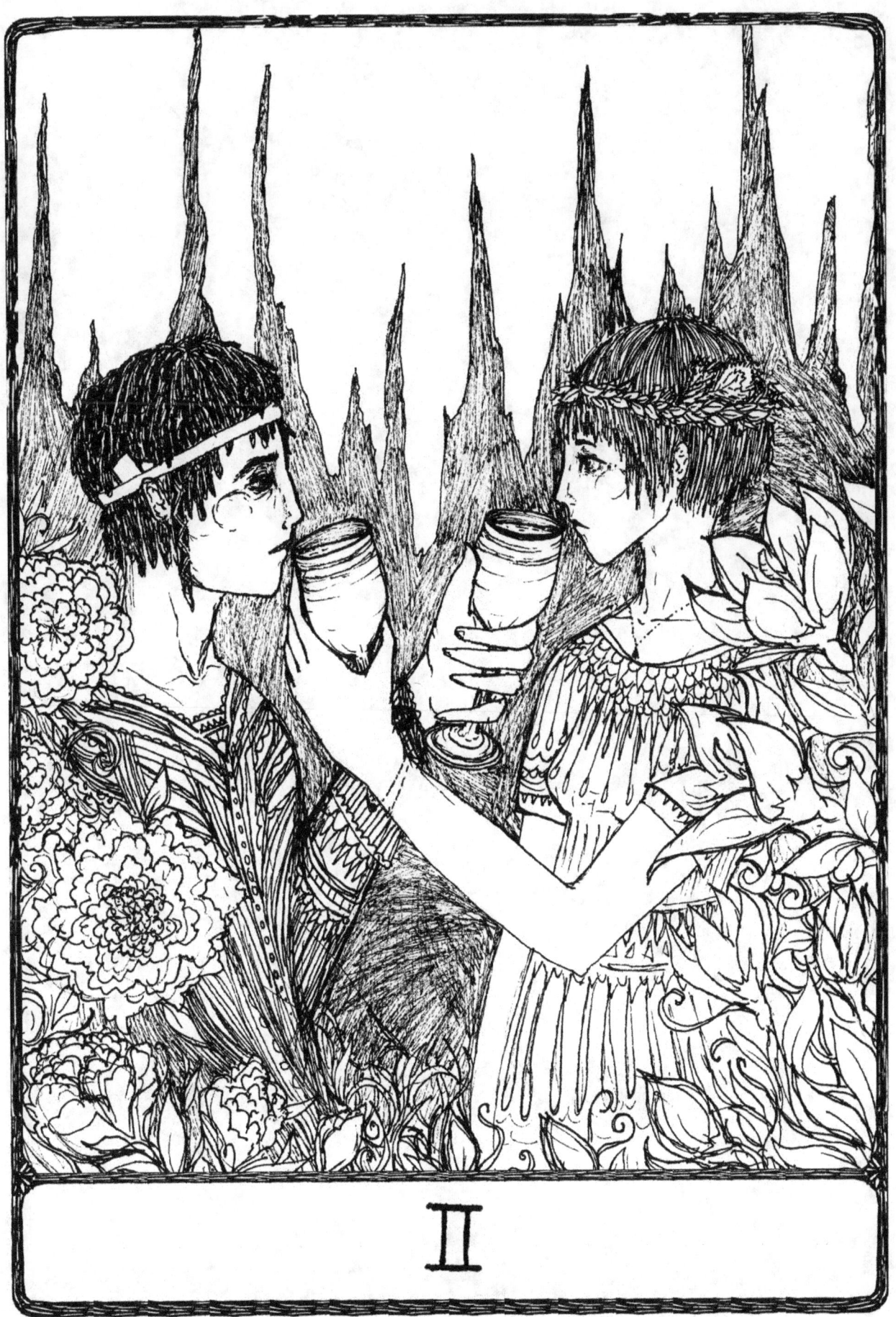

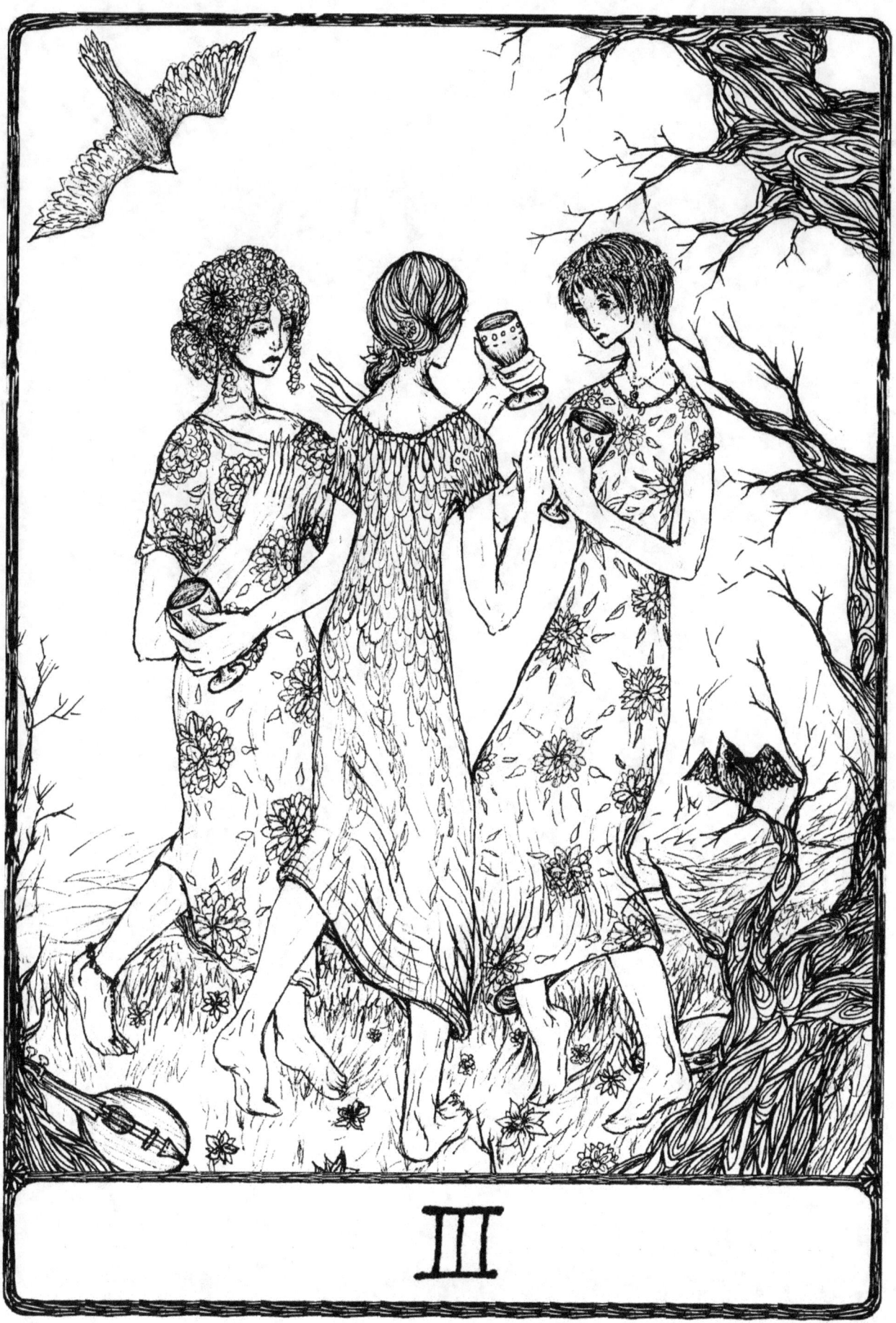

III

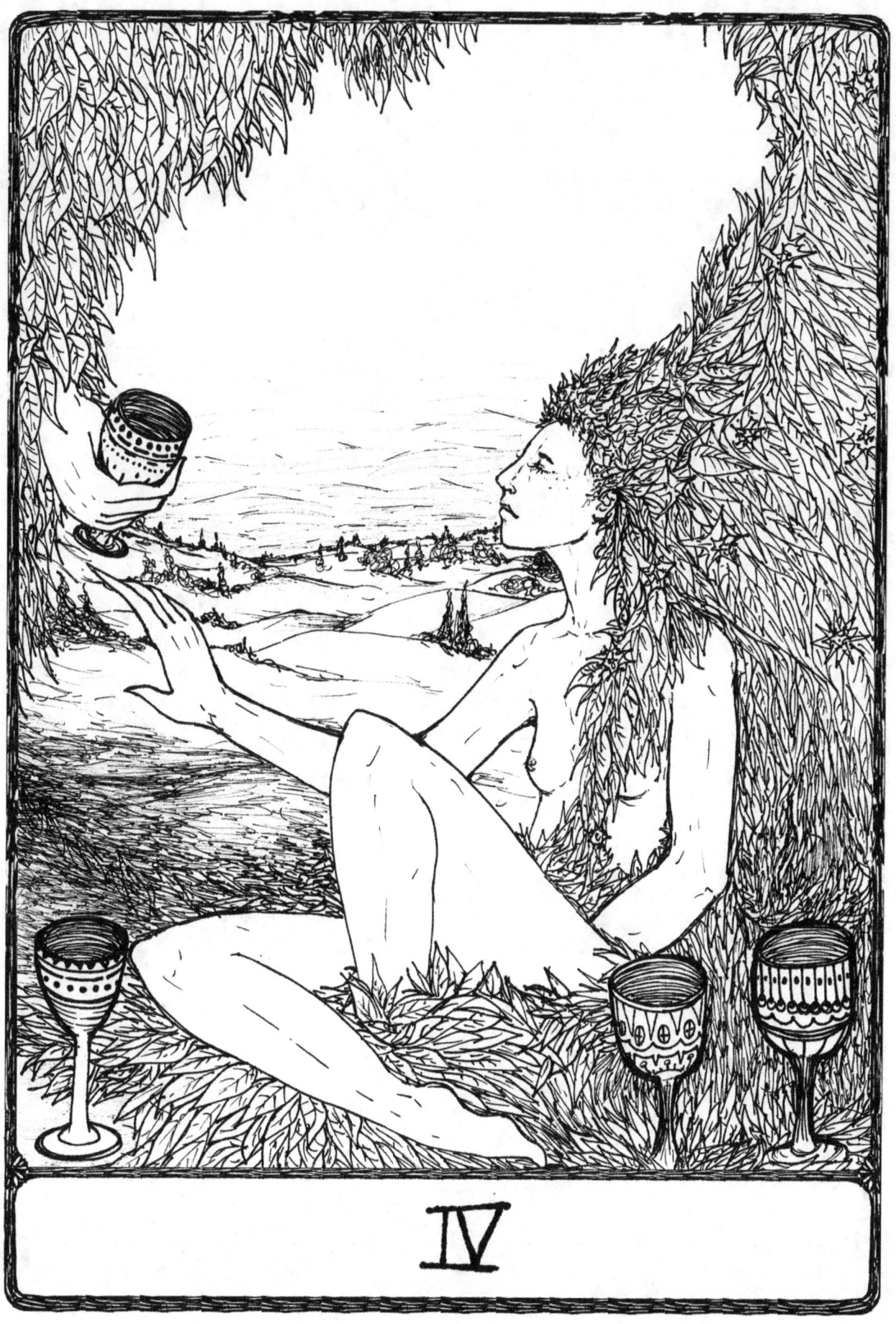

IV

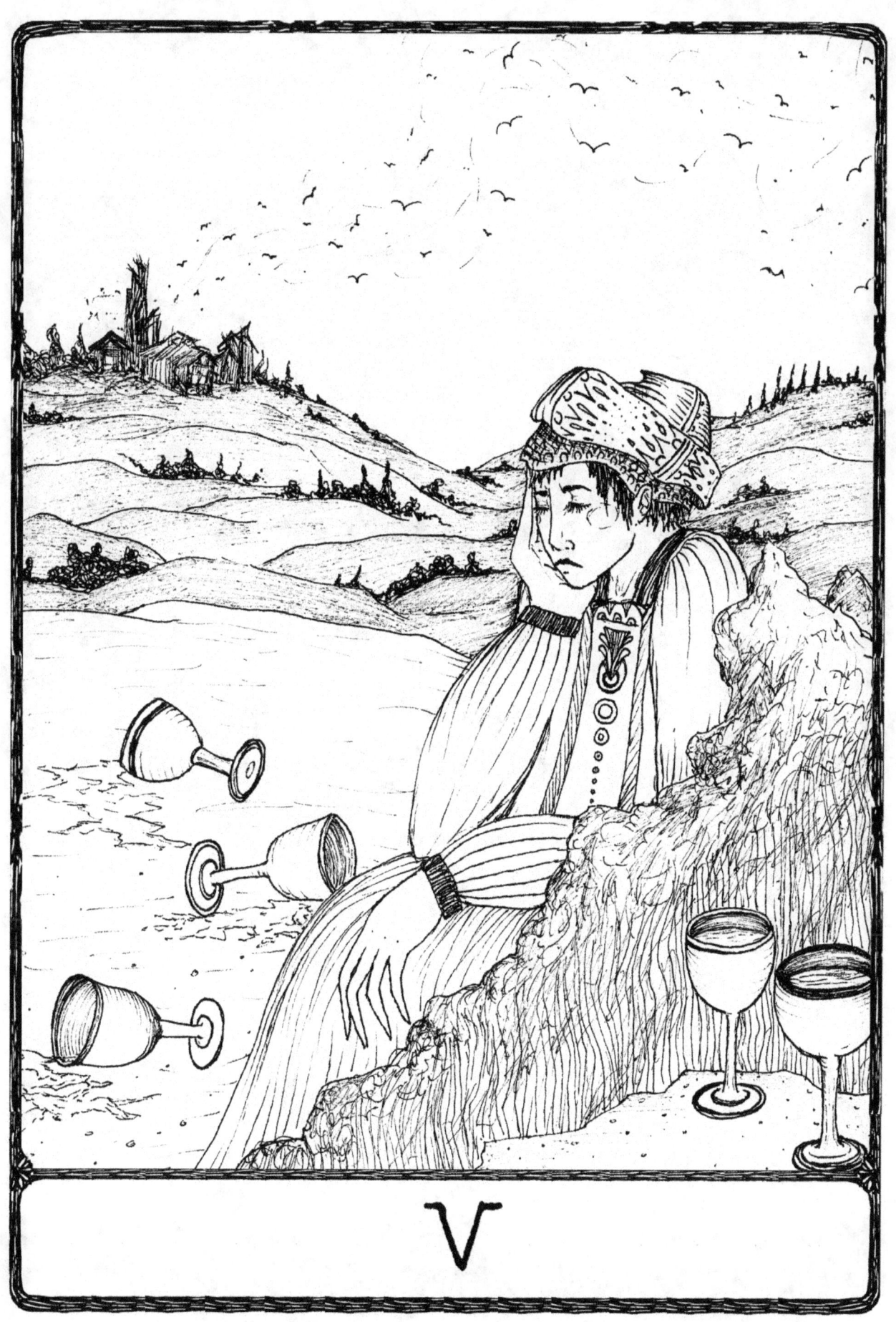

V

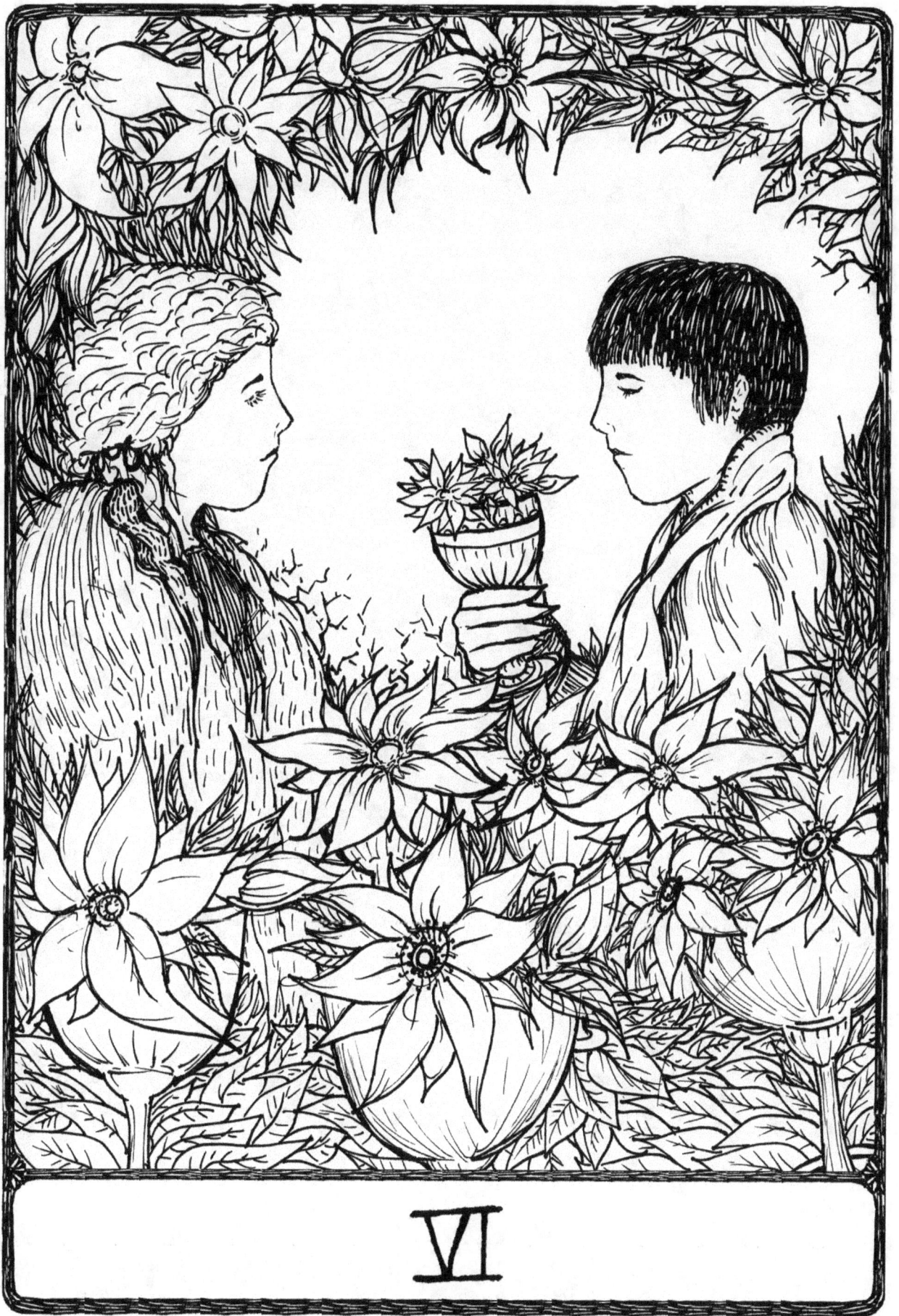

VI

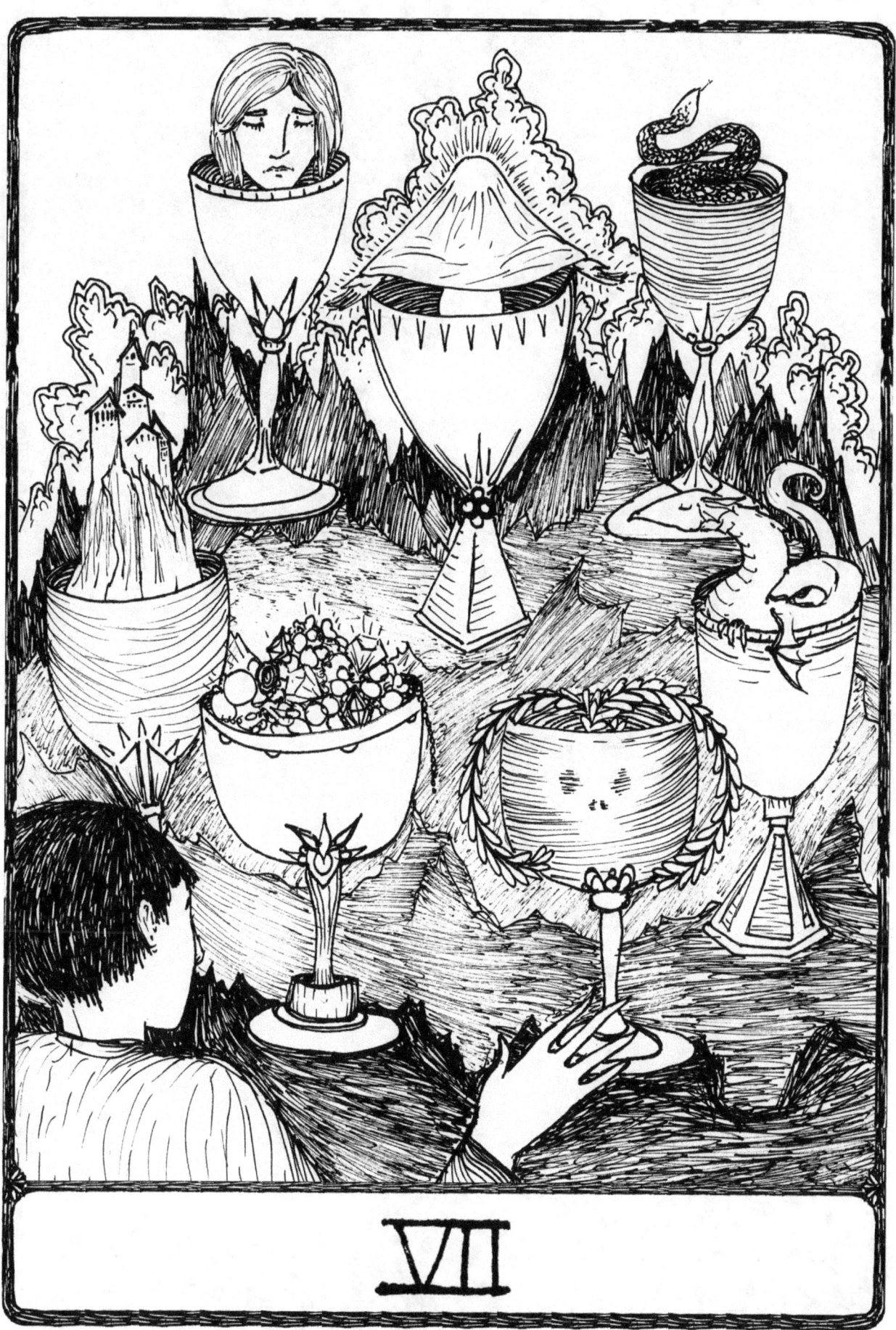

VII

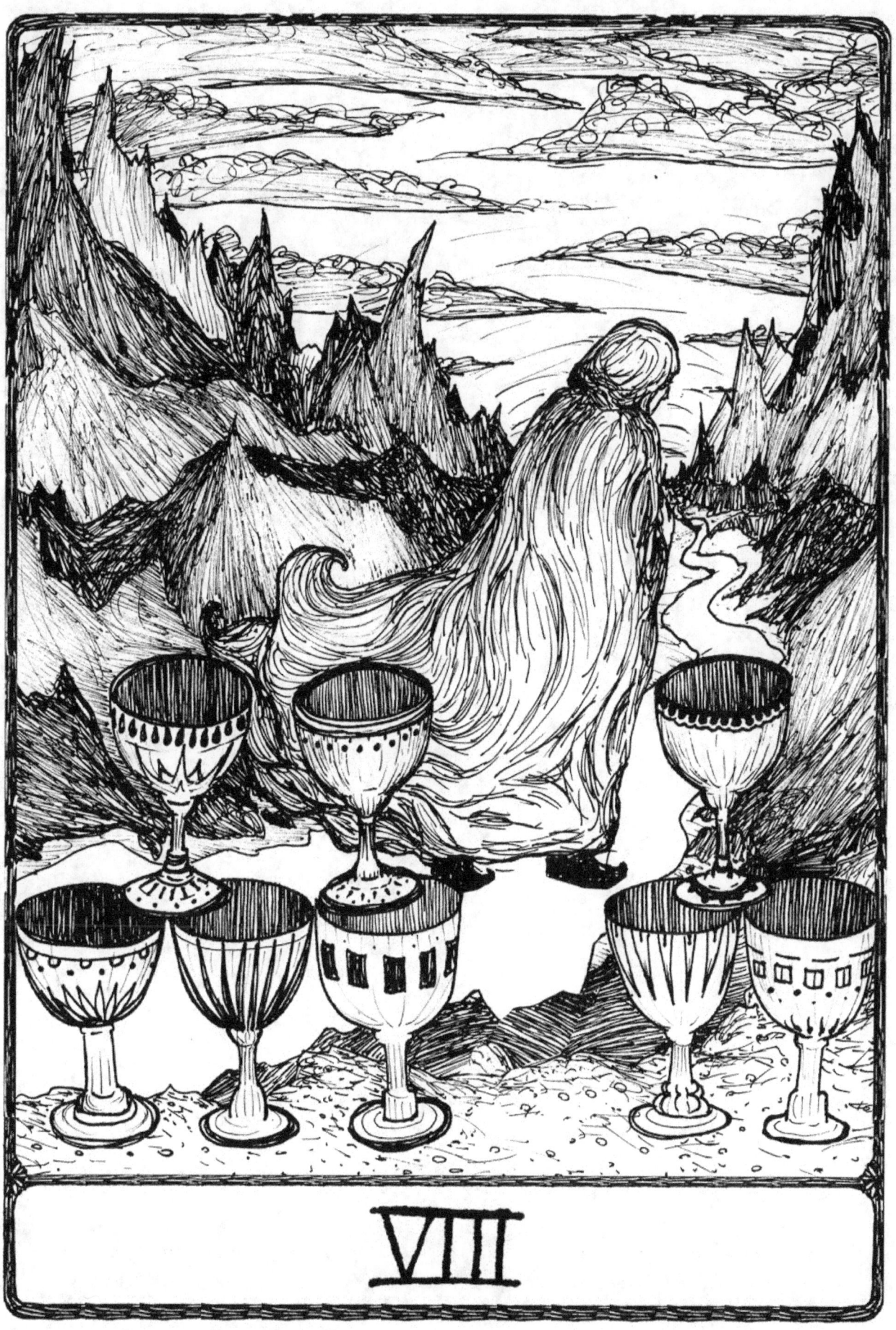

VIII

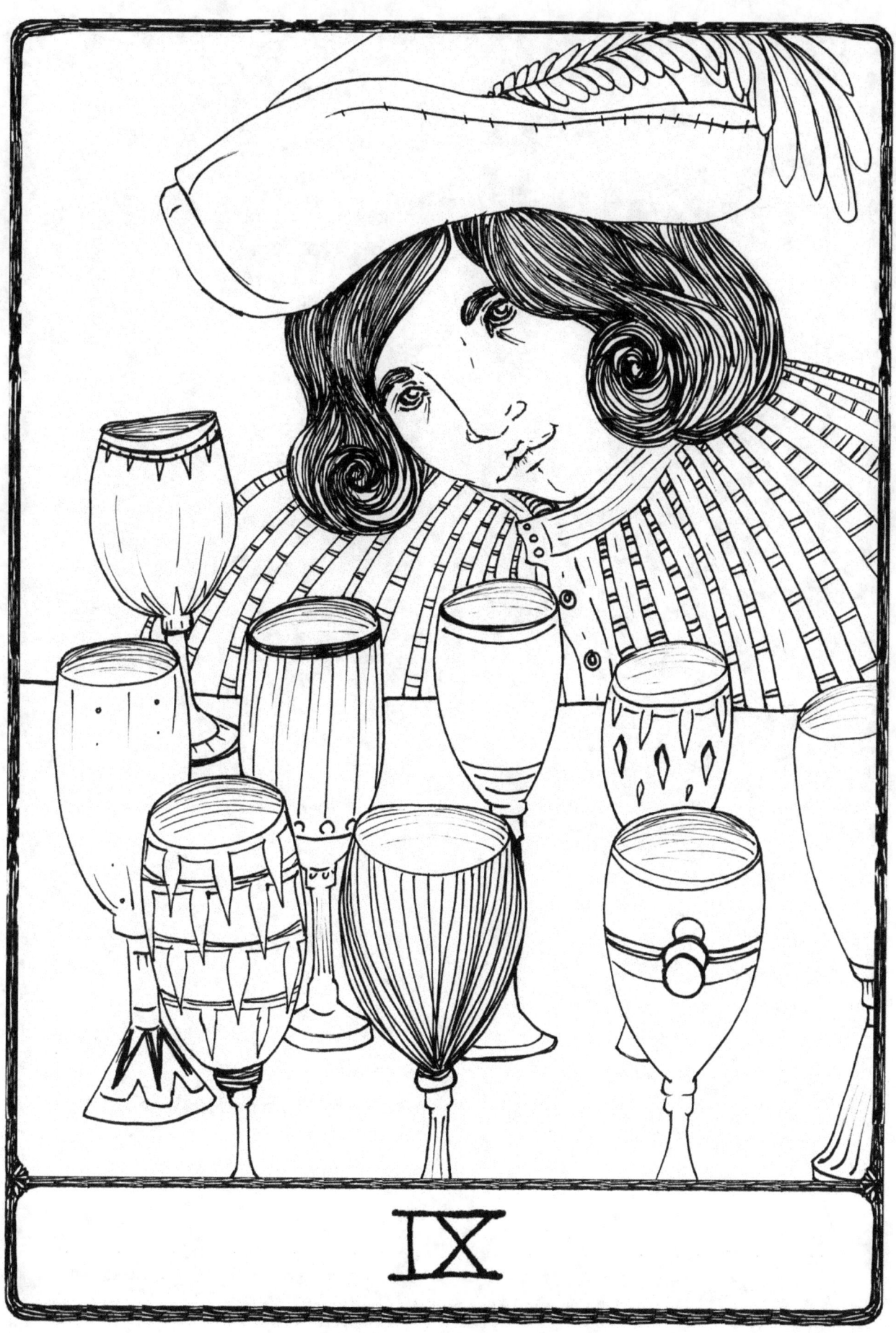

IX

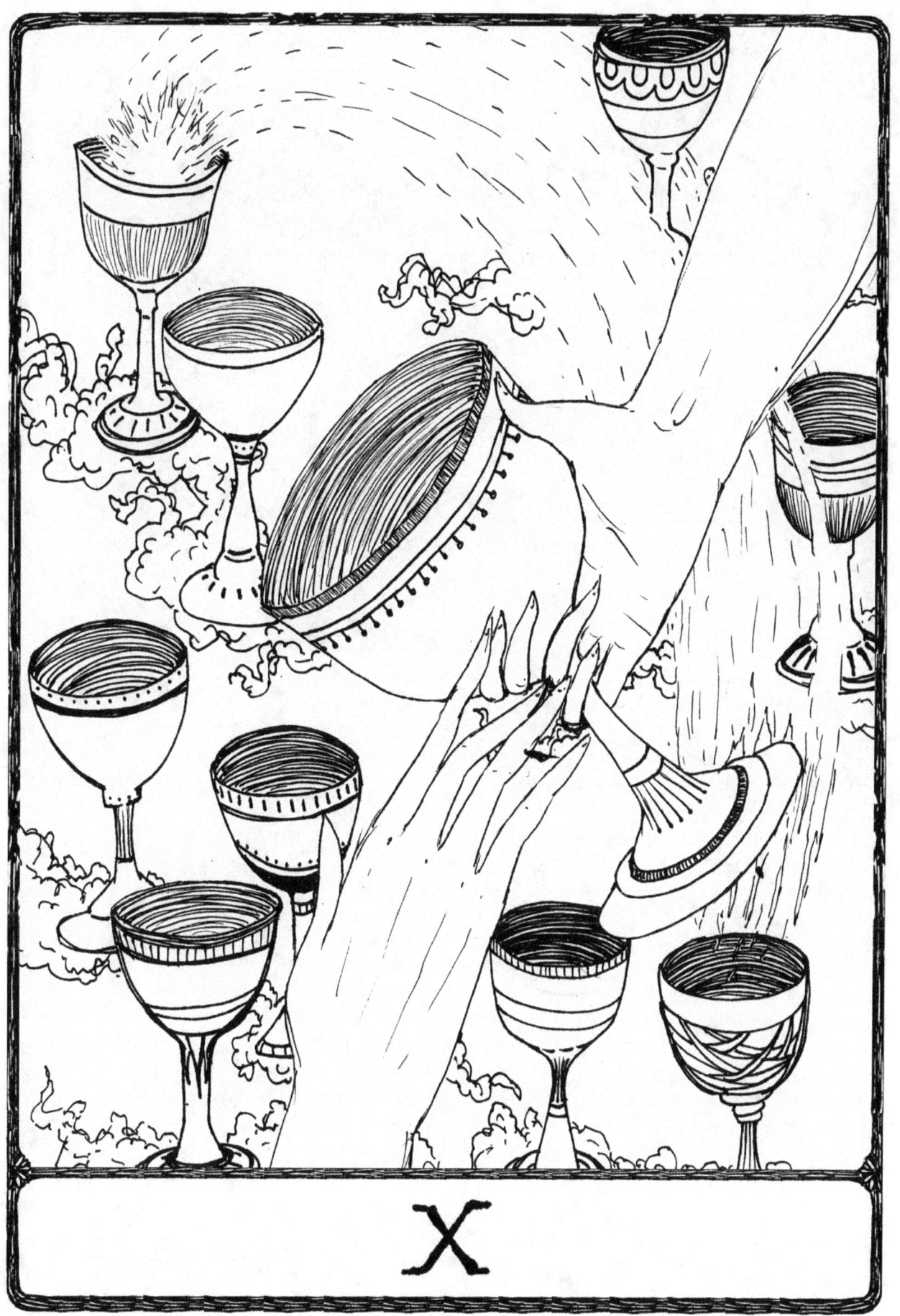

X

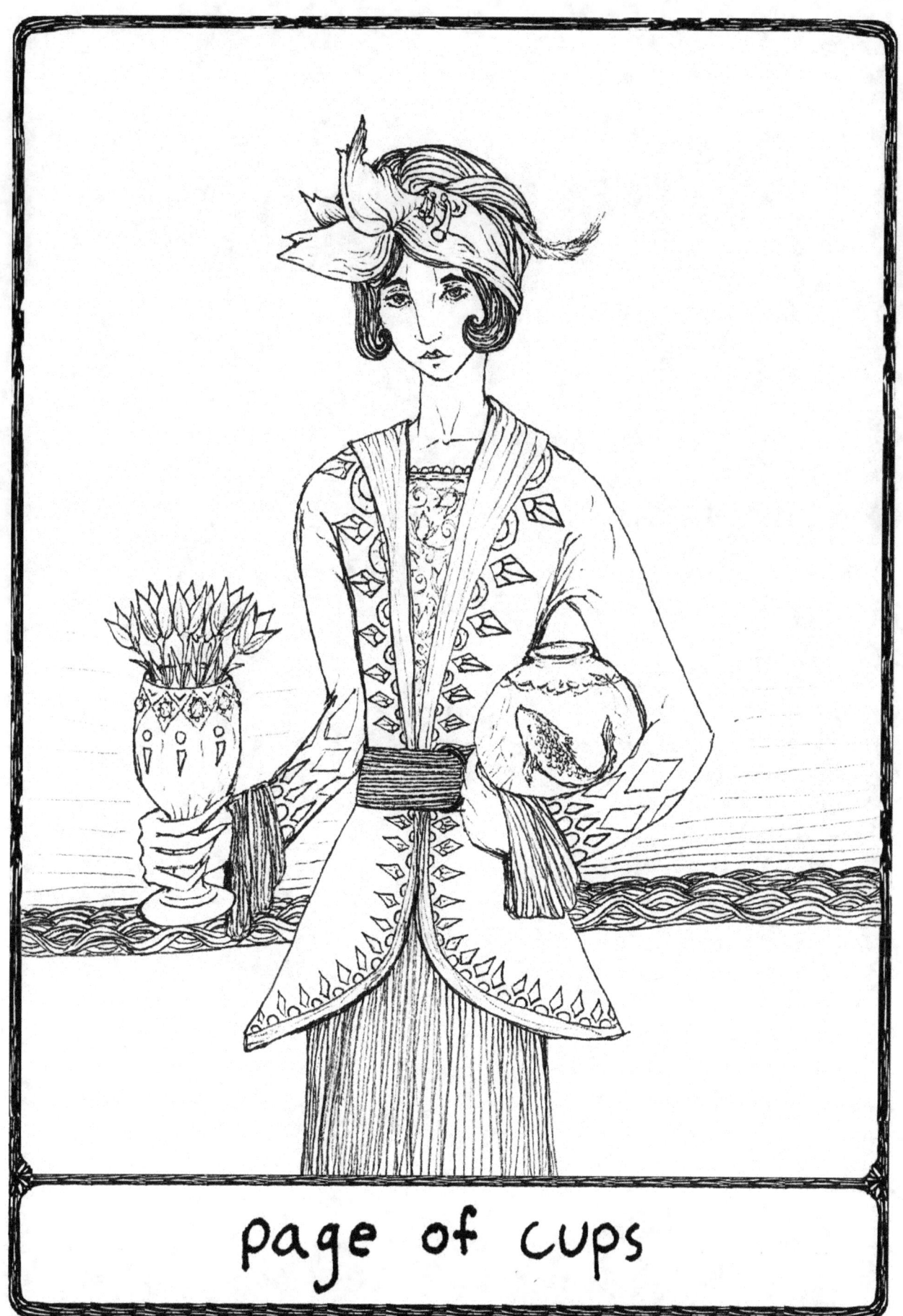

page of cups

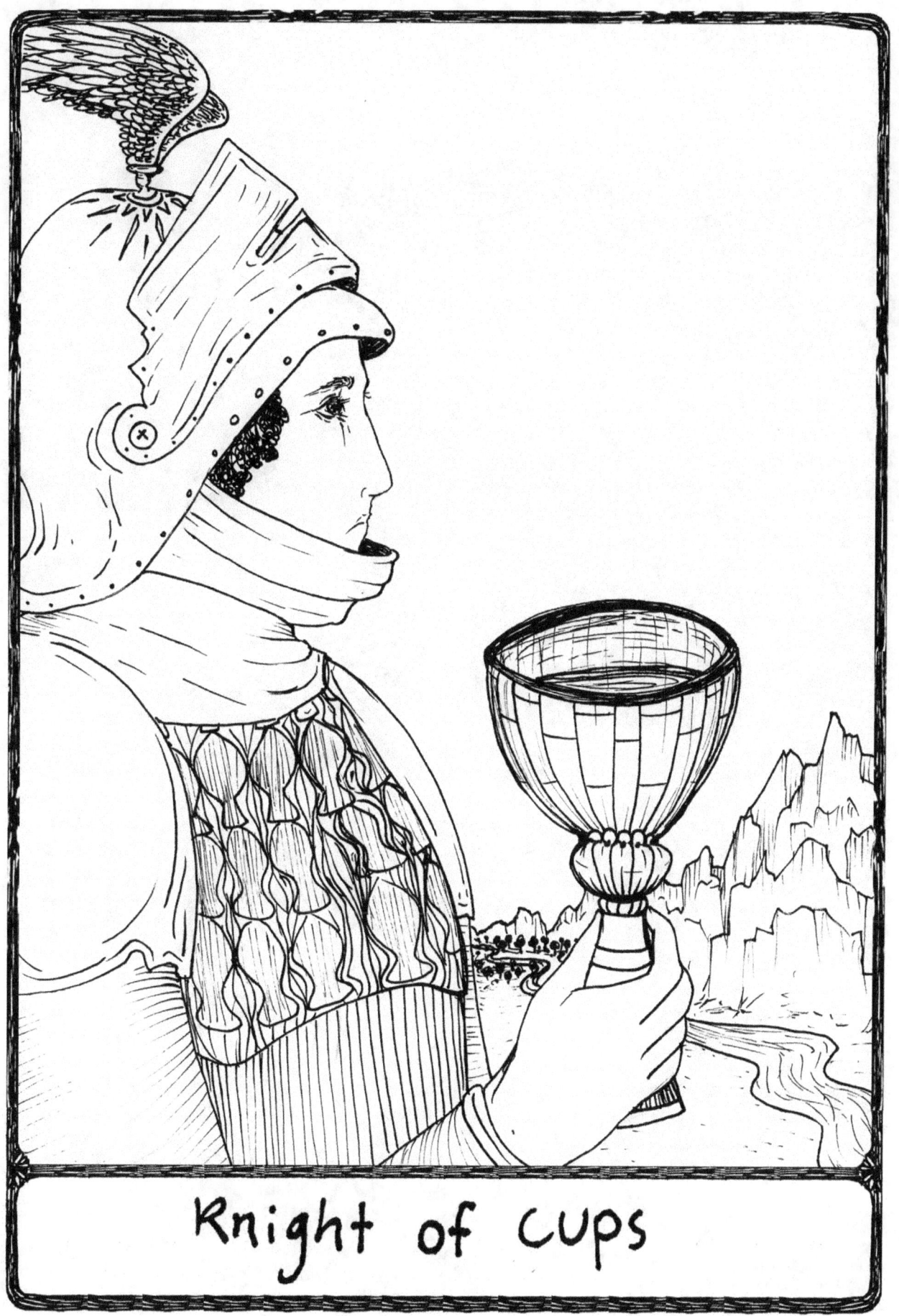

Knight of Cups

Knight of Cups

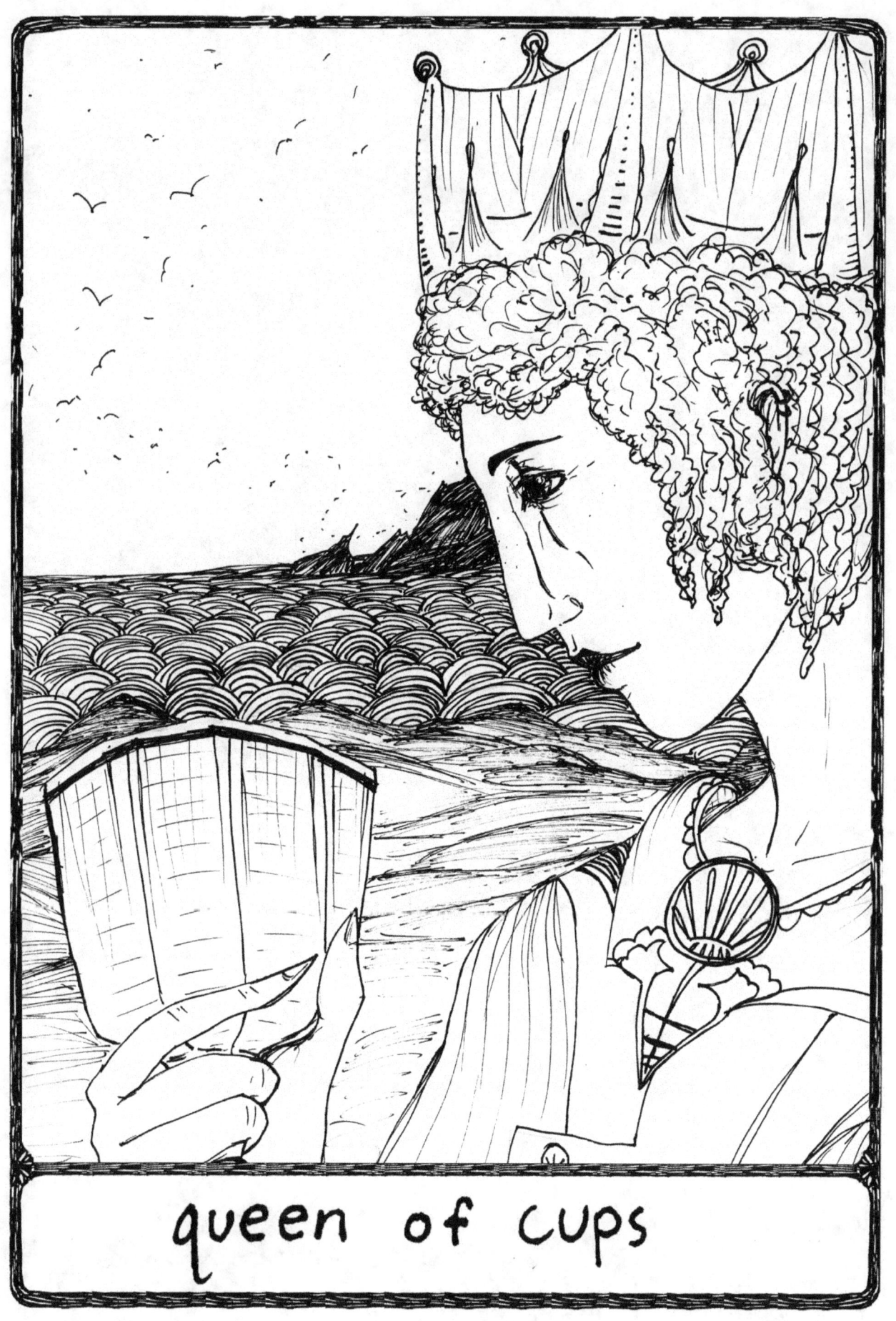

queen of cups

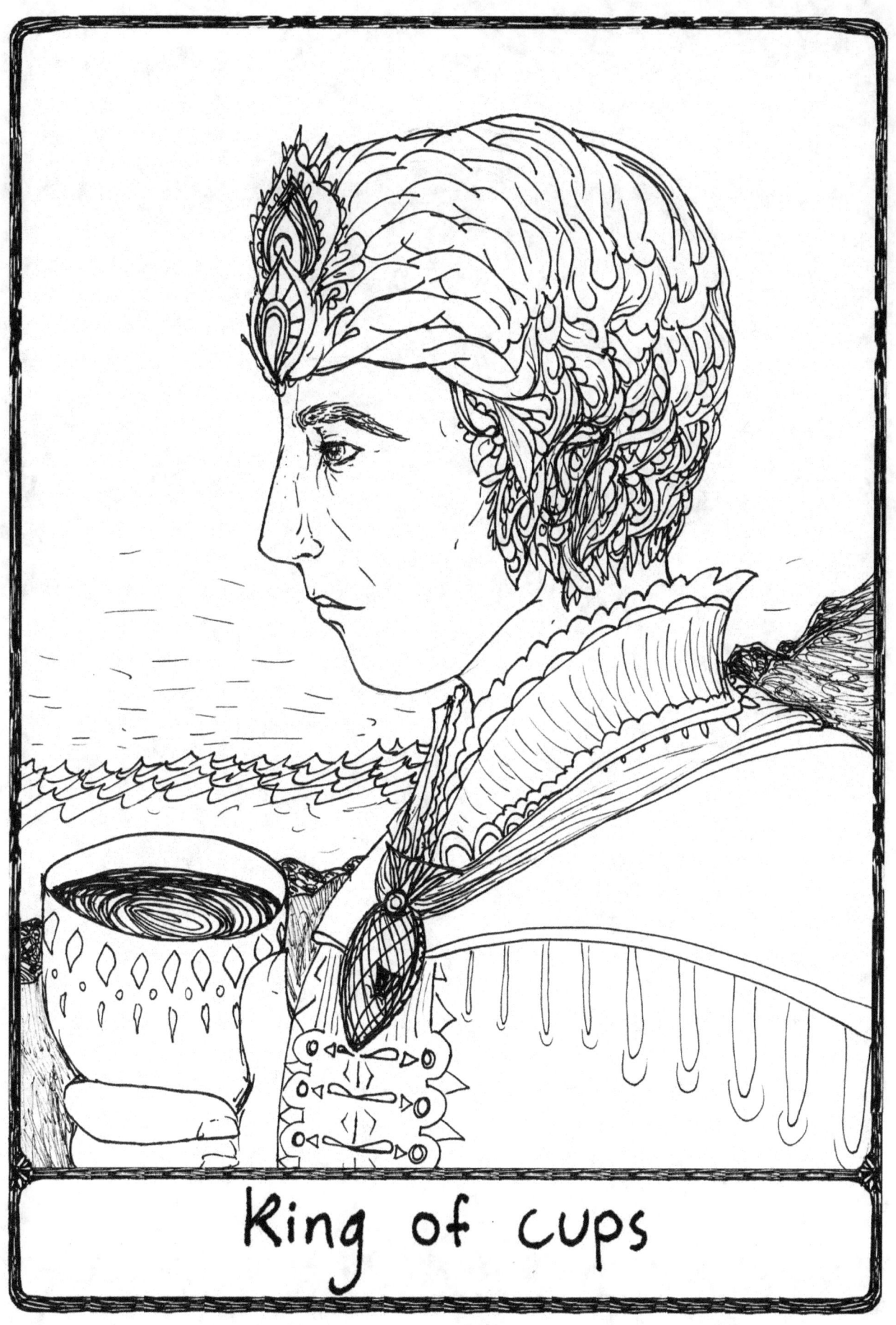

King of cups

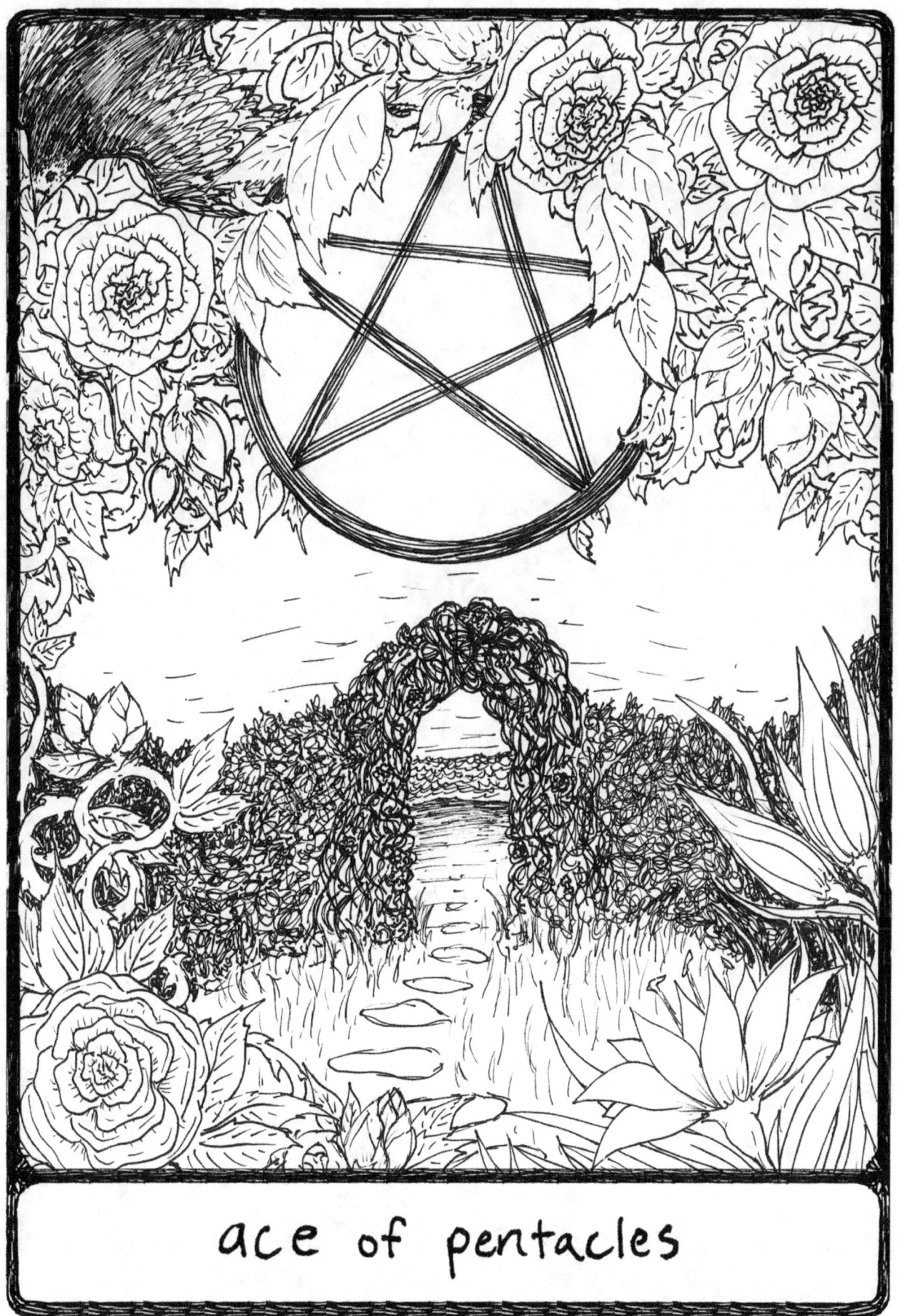

ace of pentacles

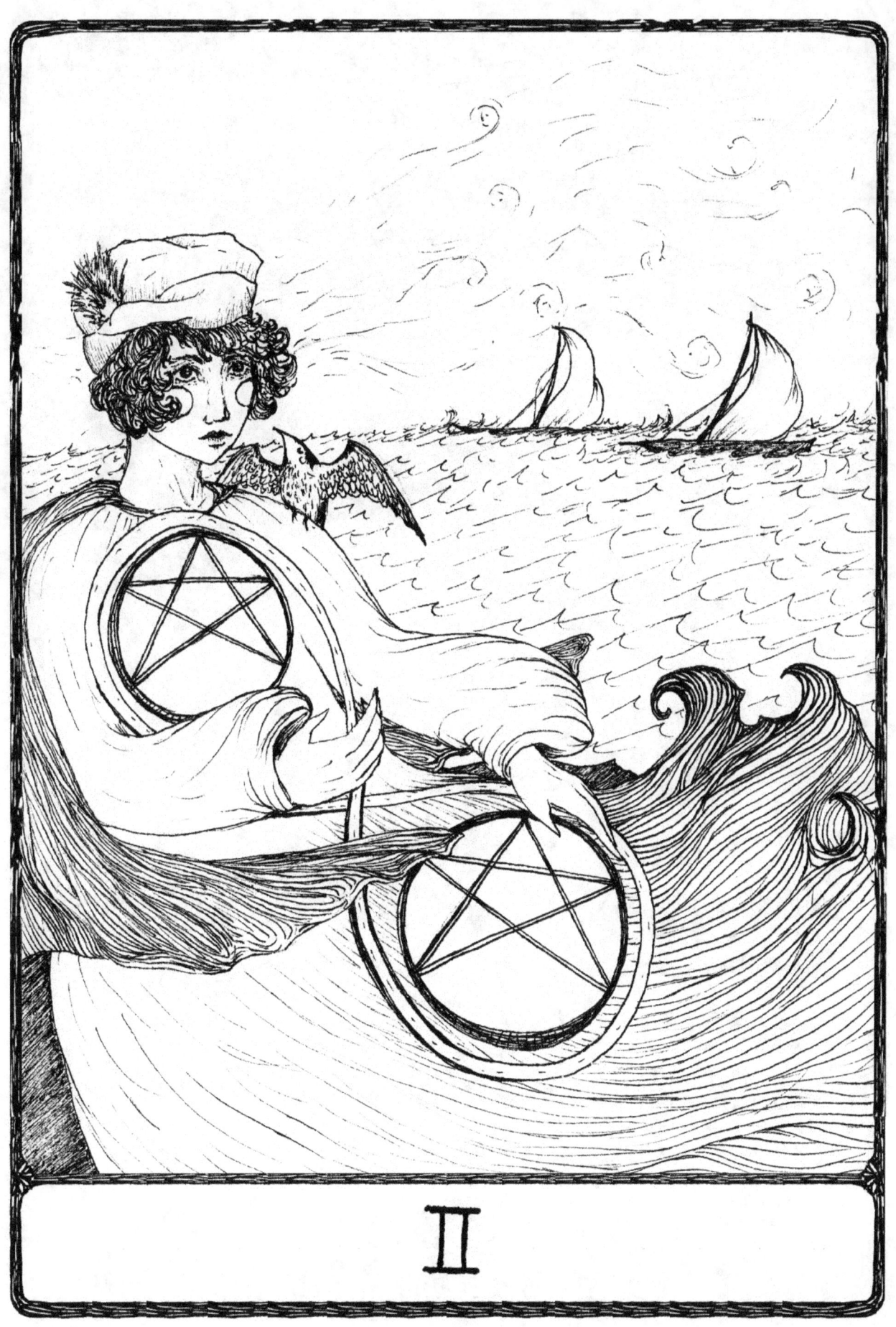

II

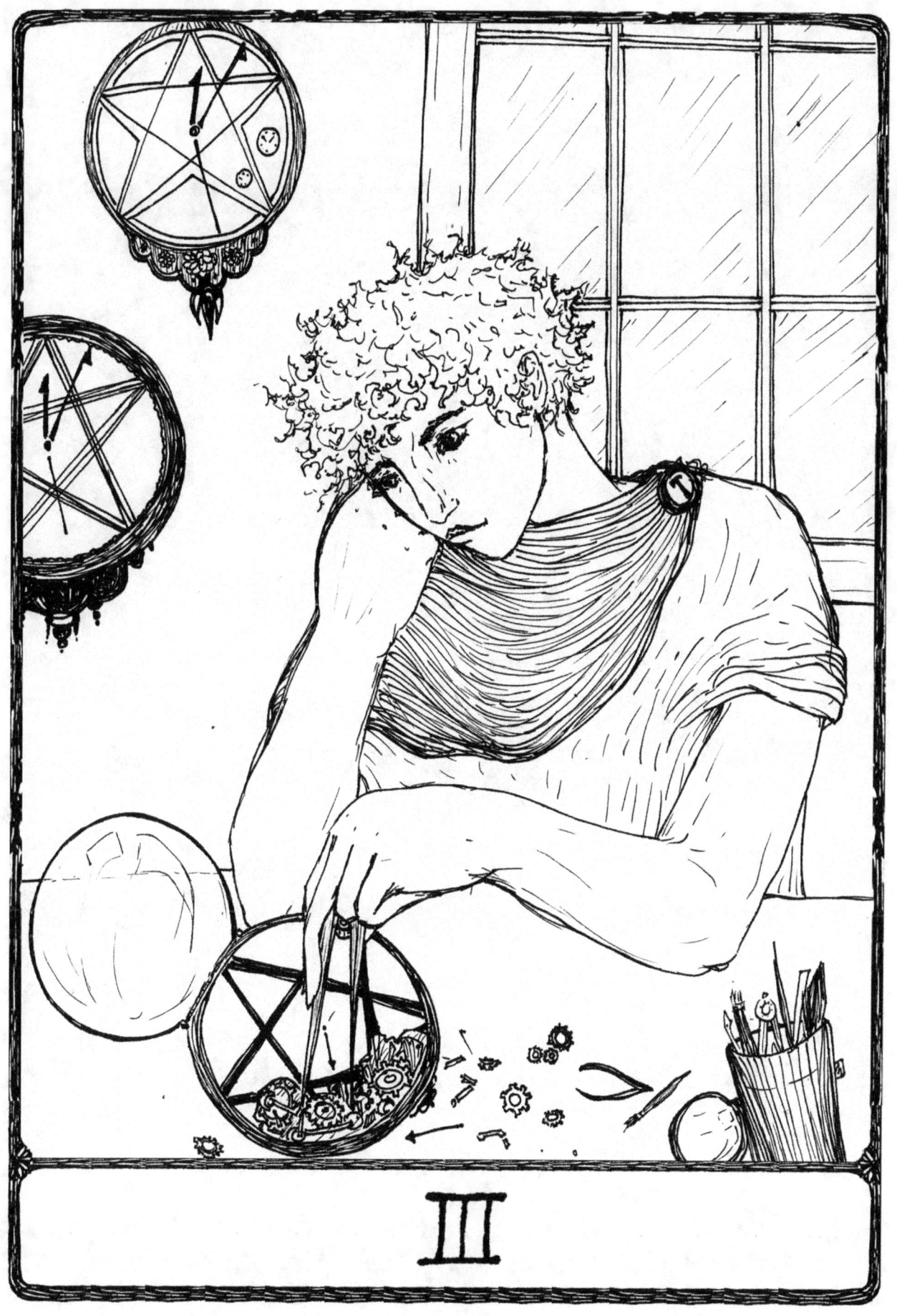

III

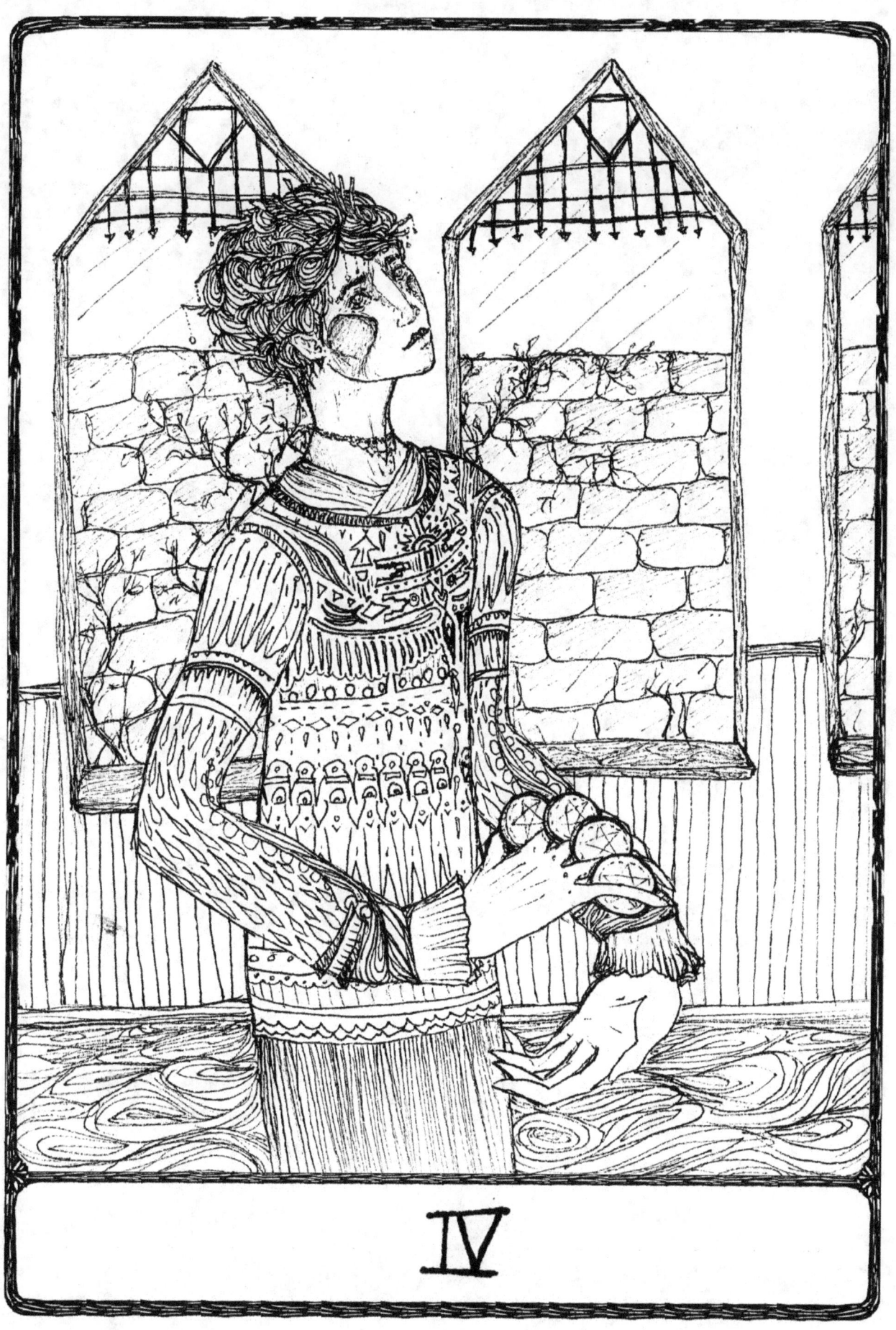

IV

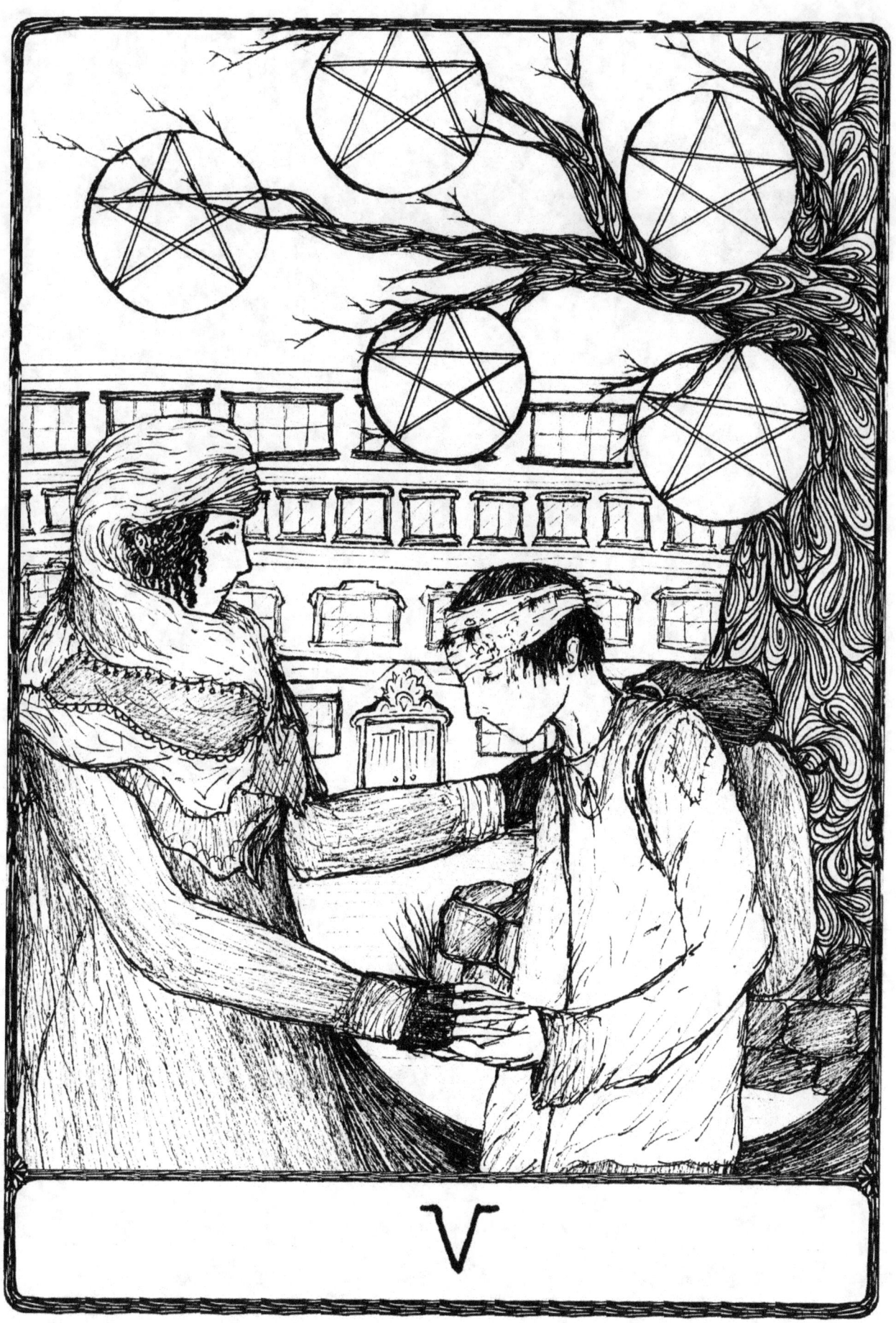

V

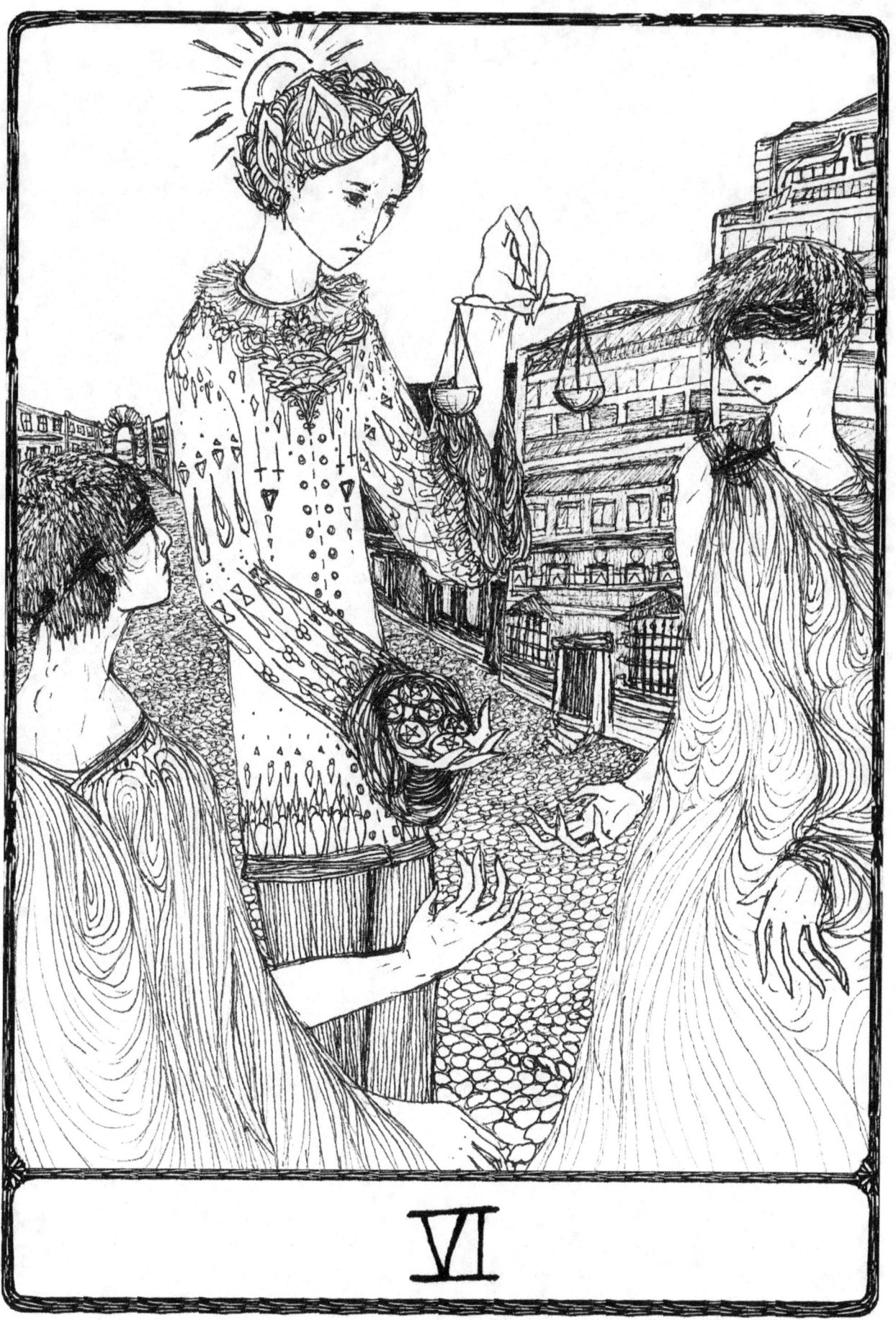

VI

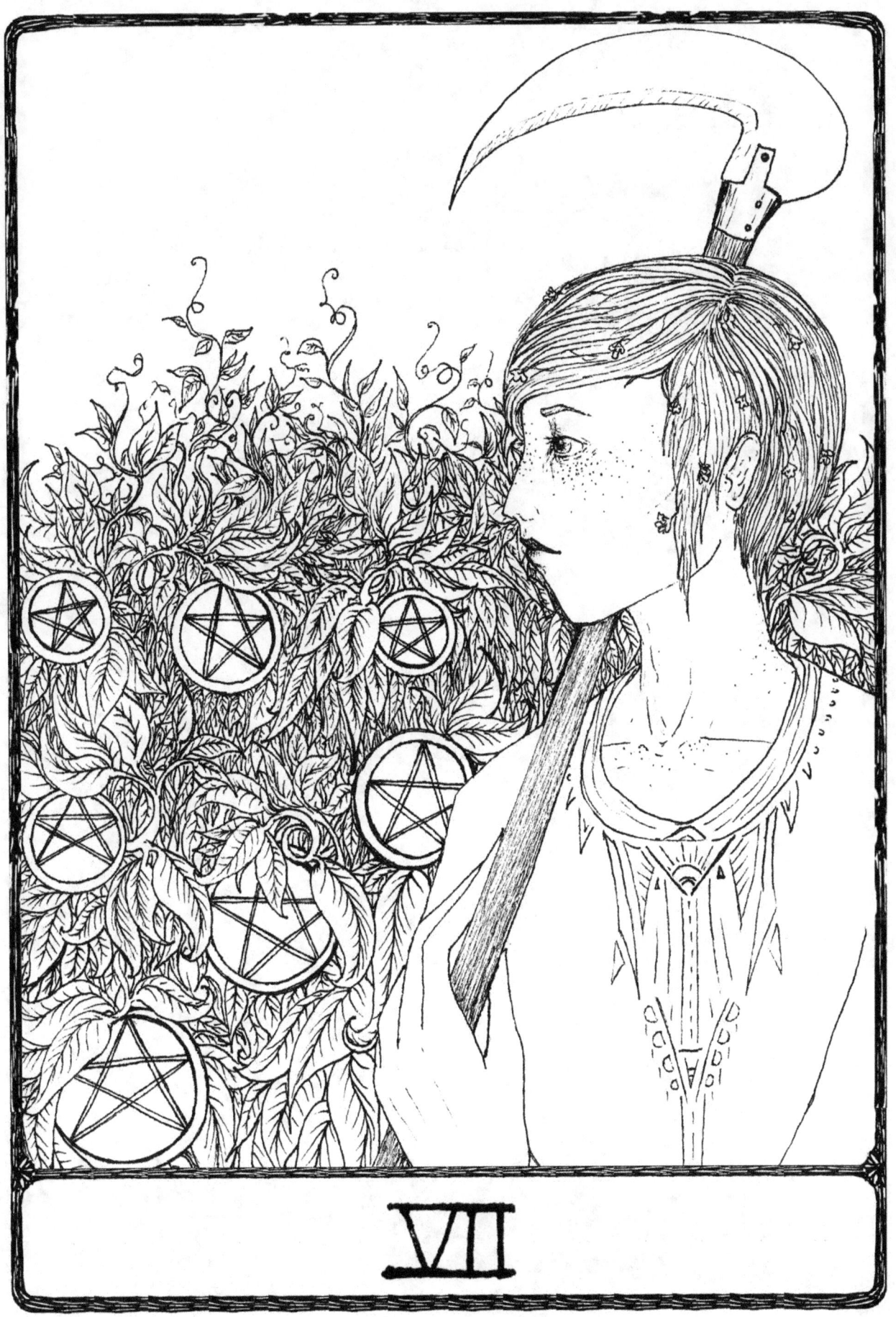

VII

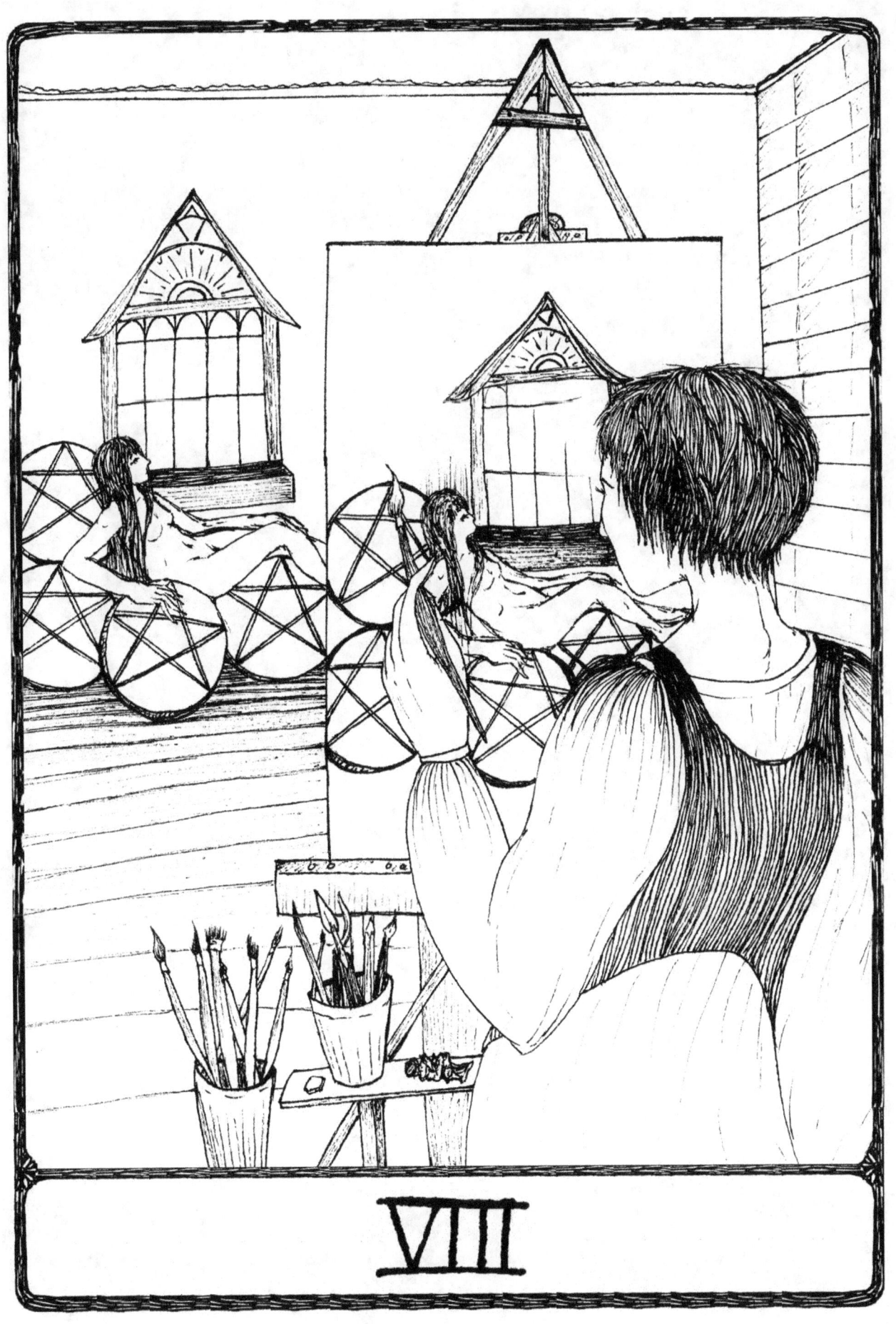

VIII

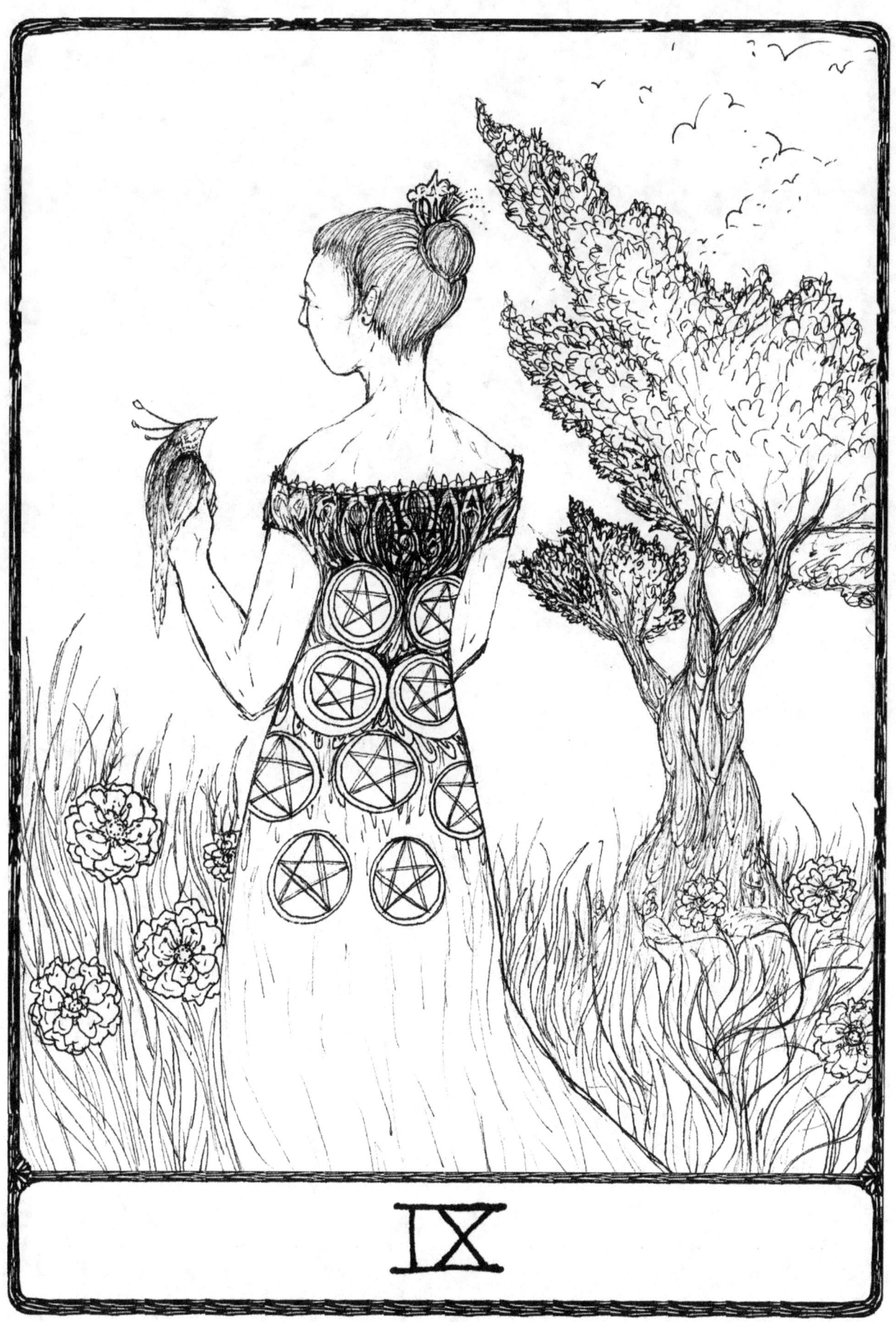

IX

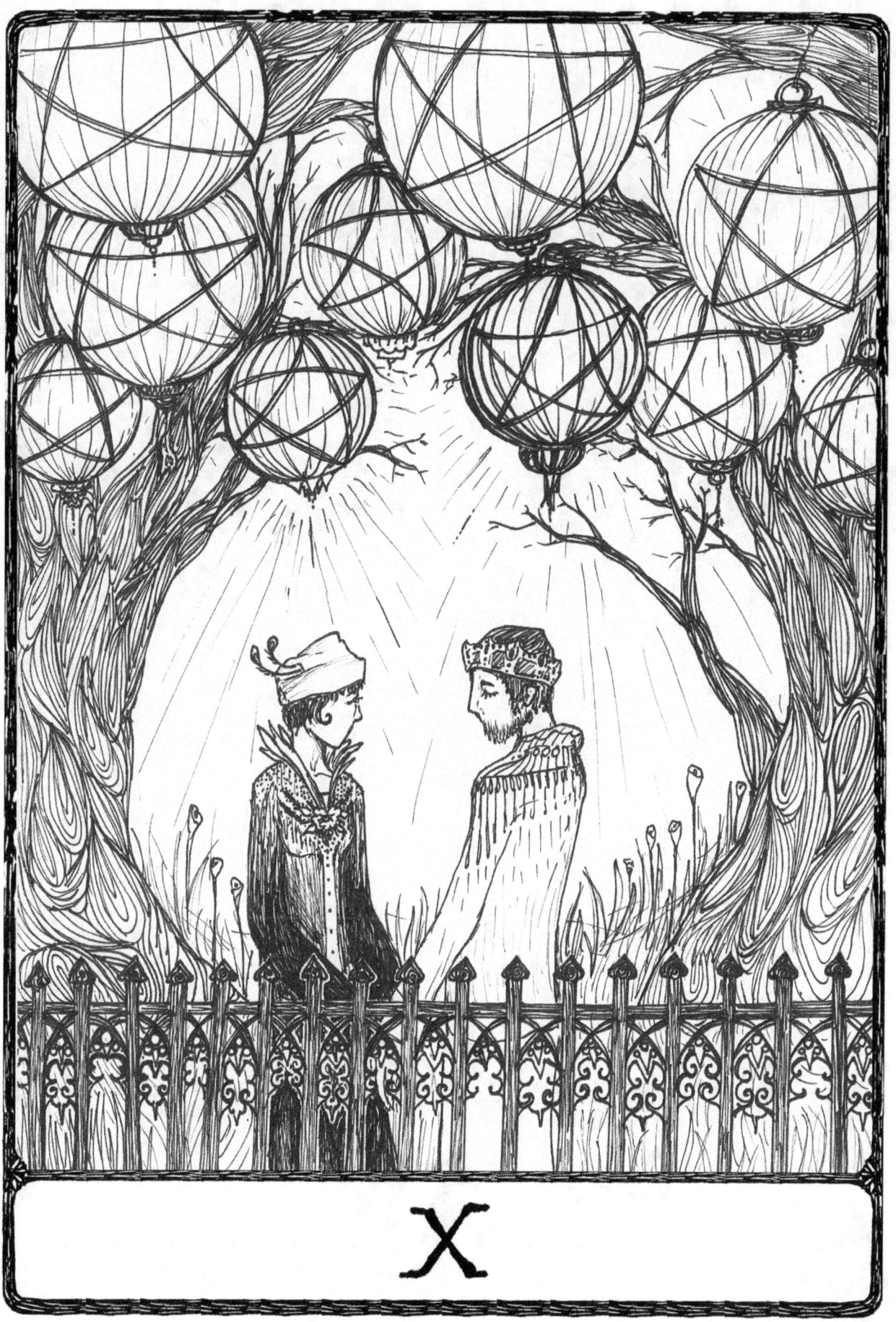

X

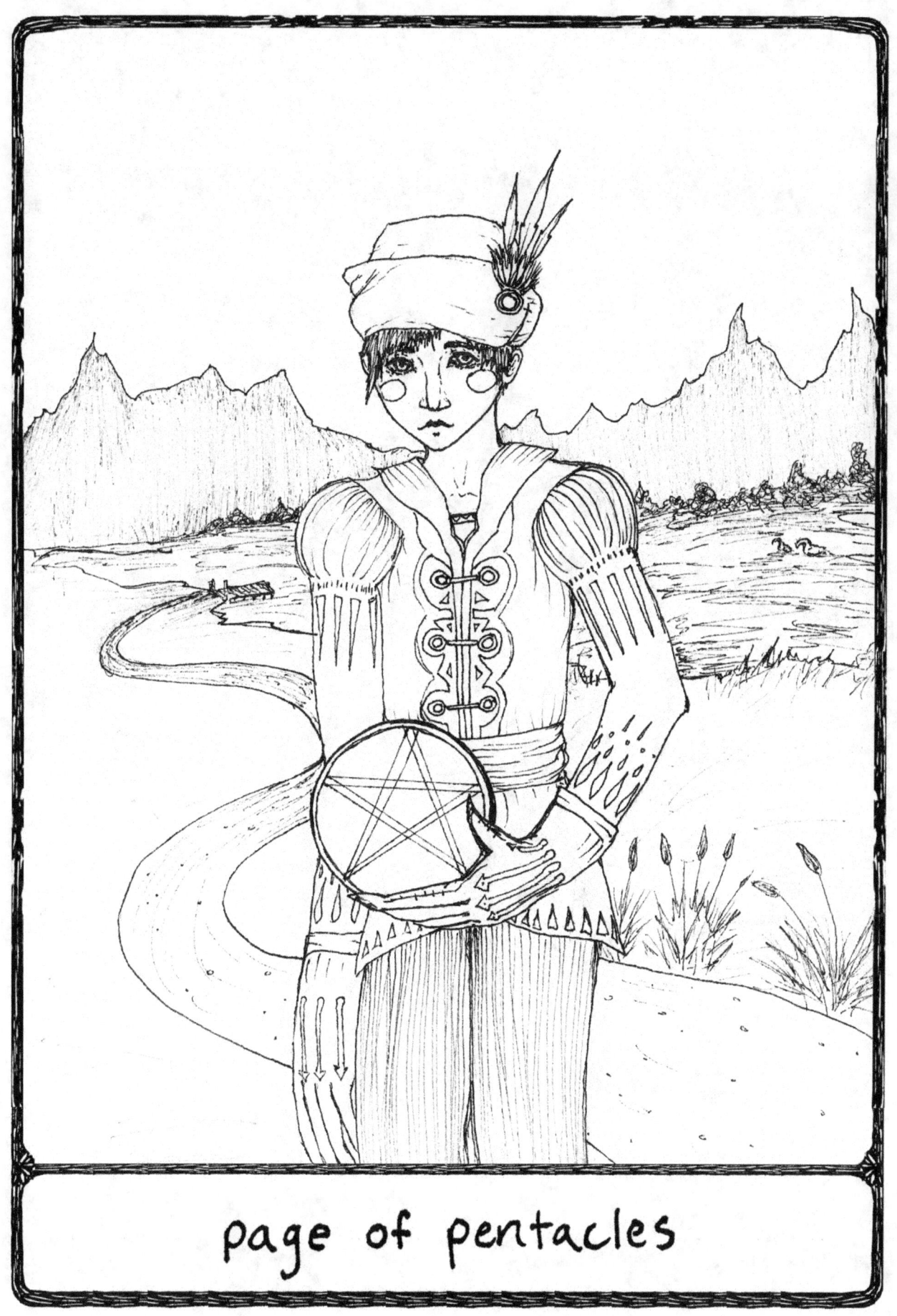

page of pentacles

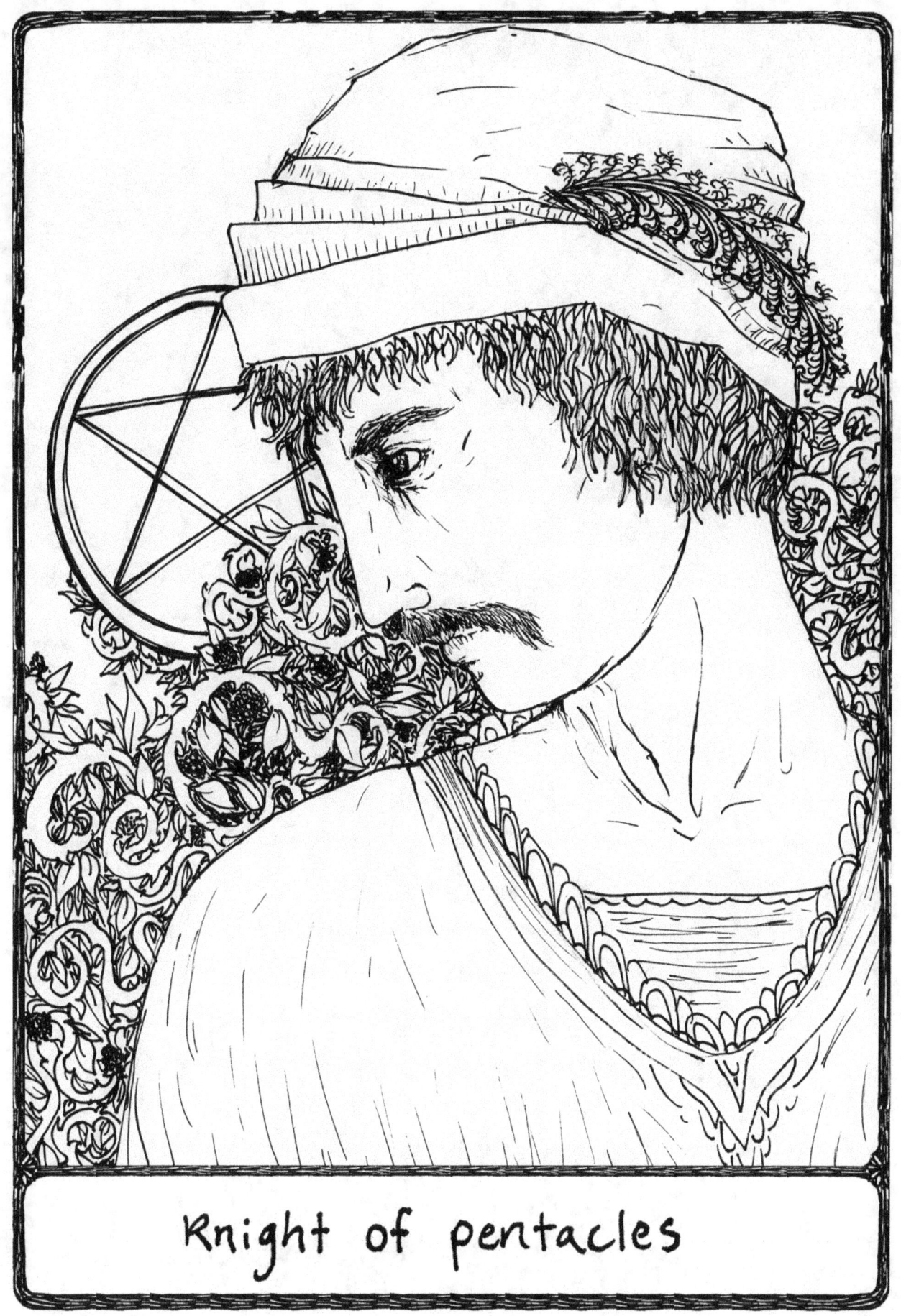

Knight of pentacles

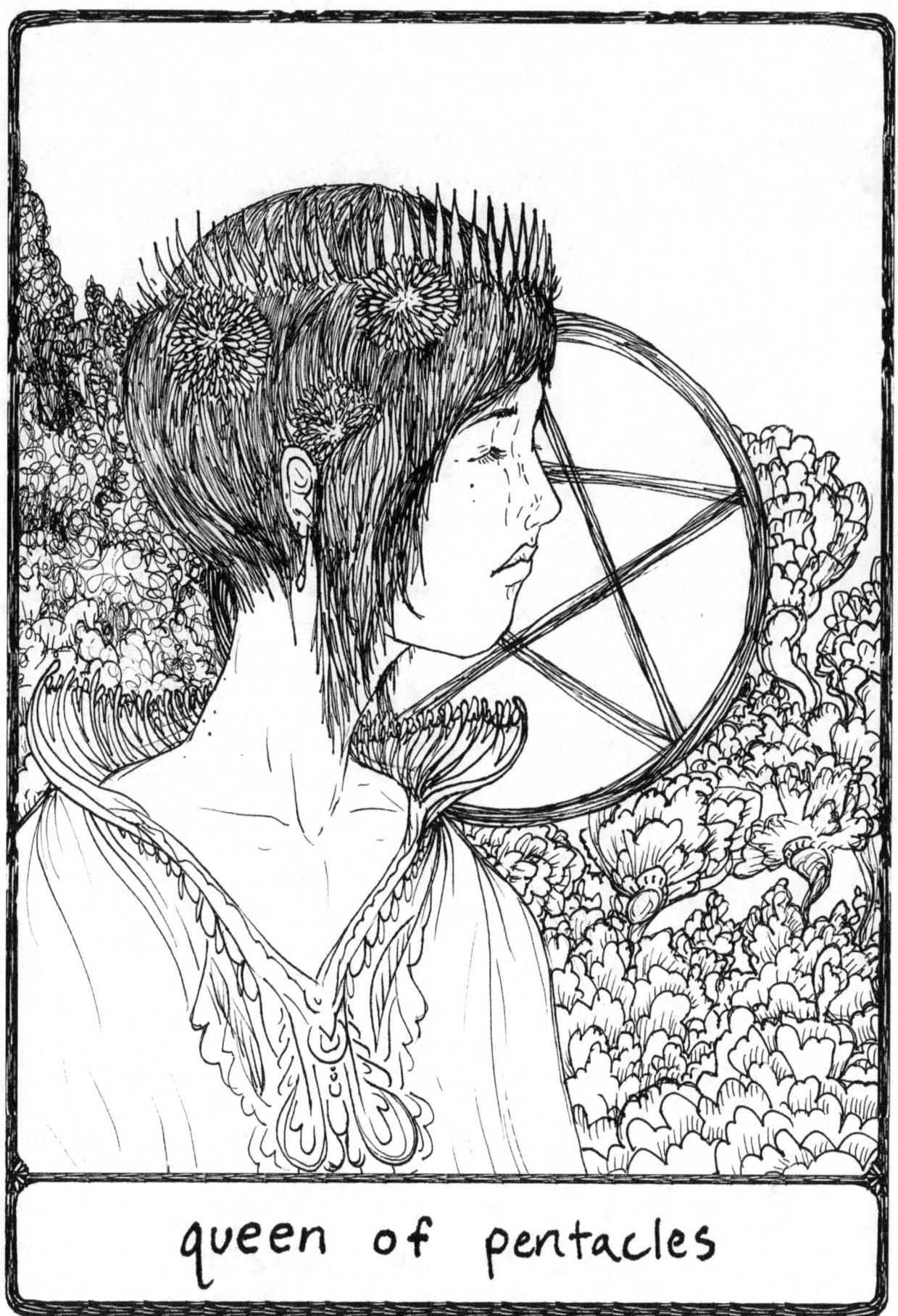

queen of pentacles

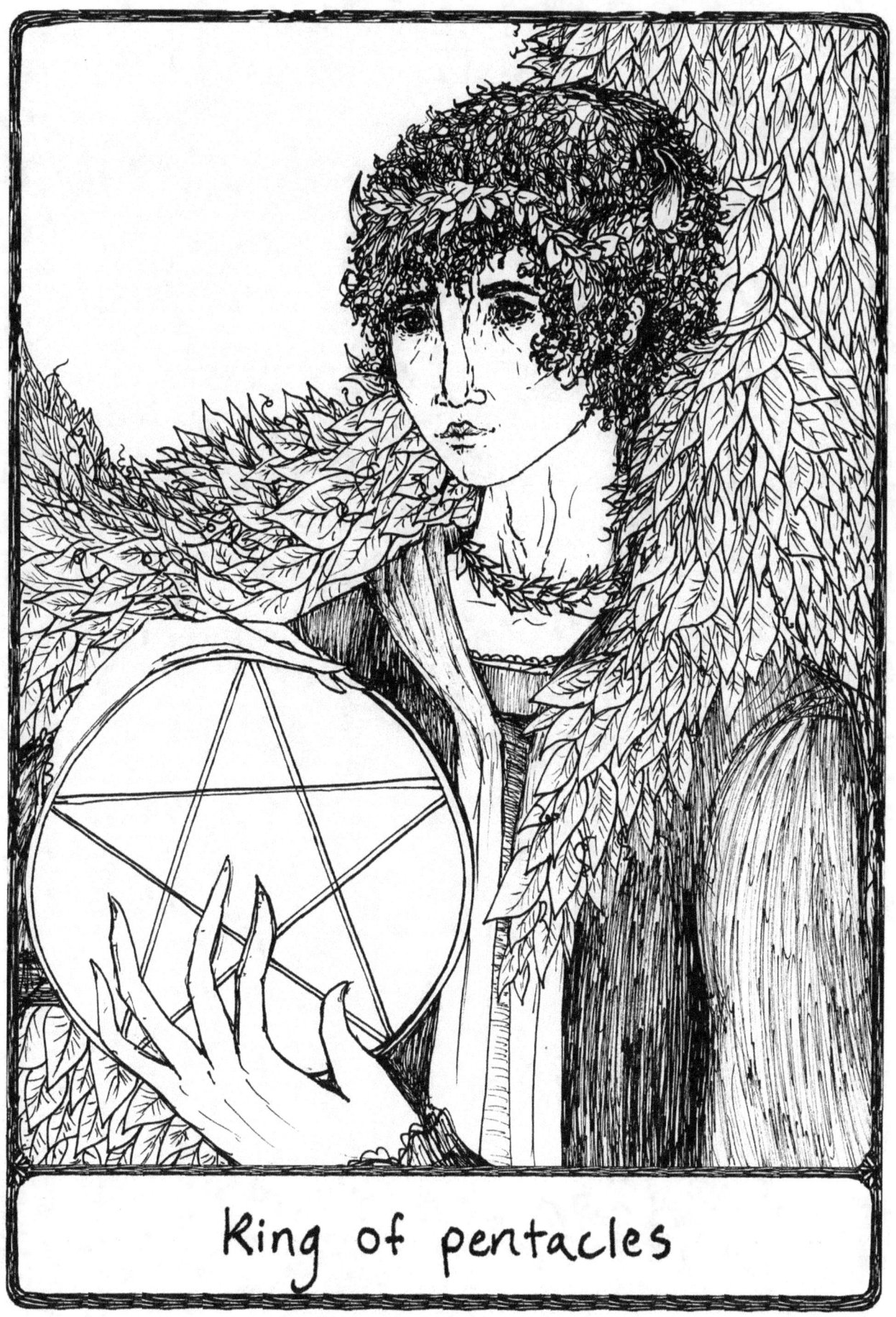

King of pentacles

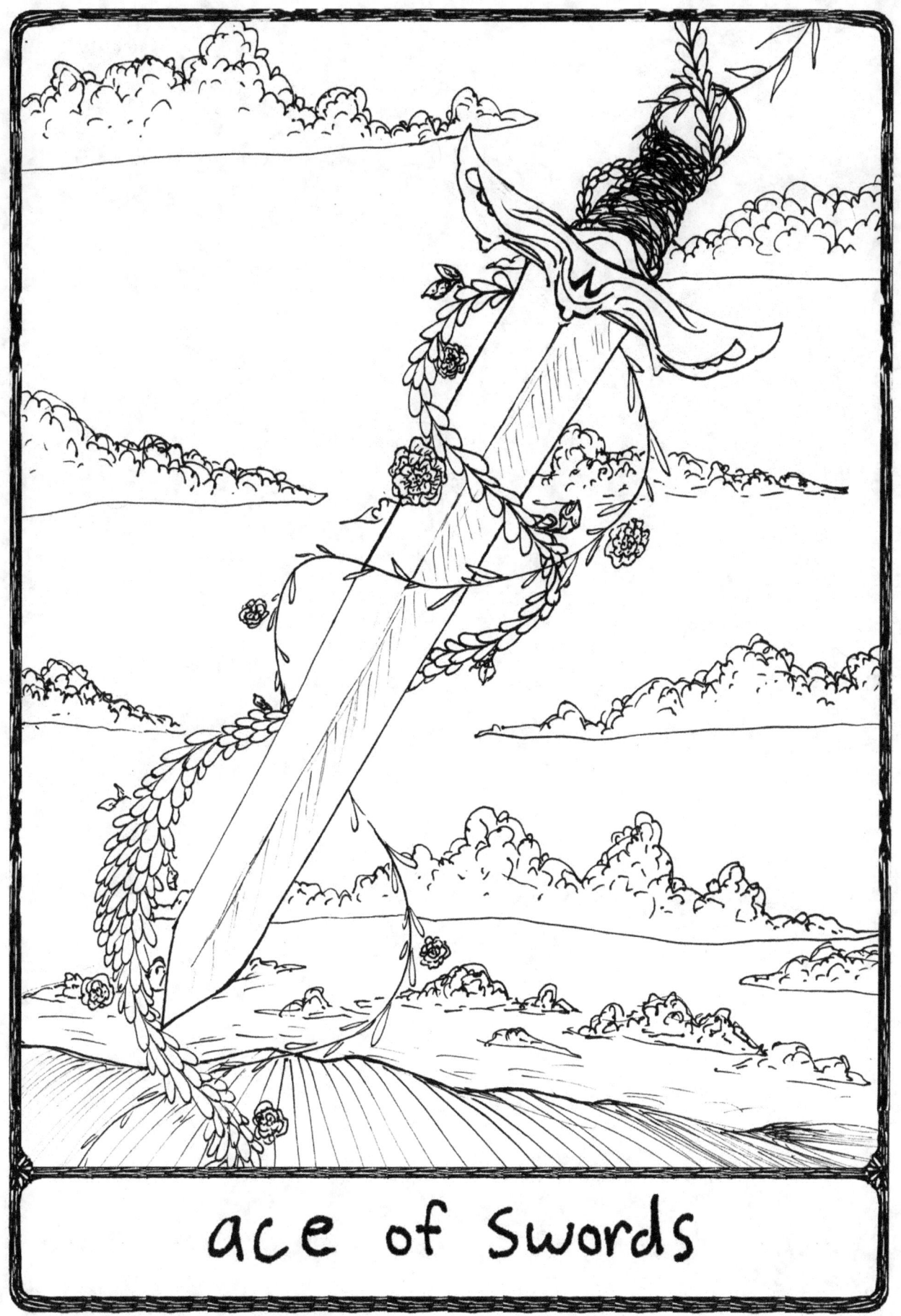

ace of swords

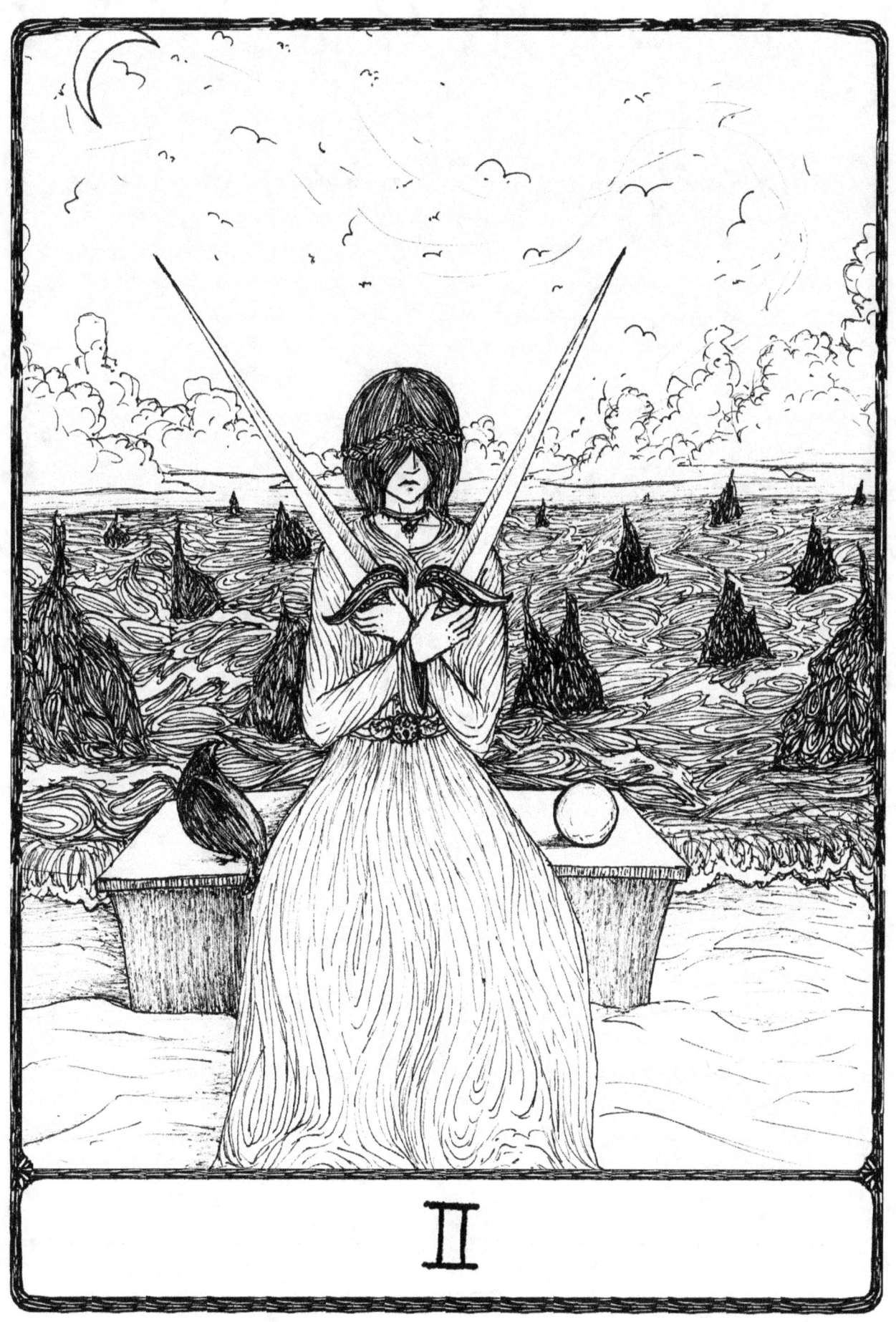

Ⅱ

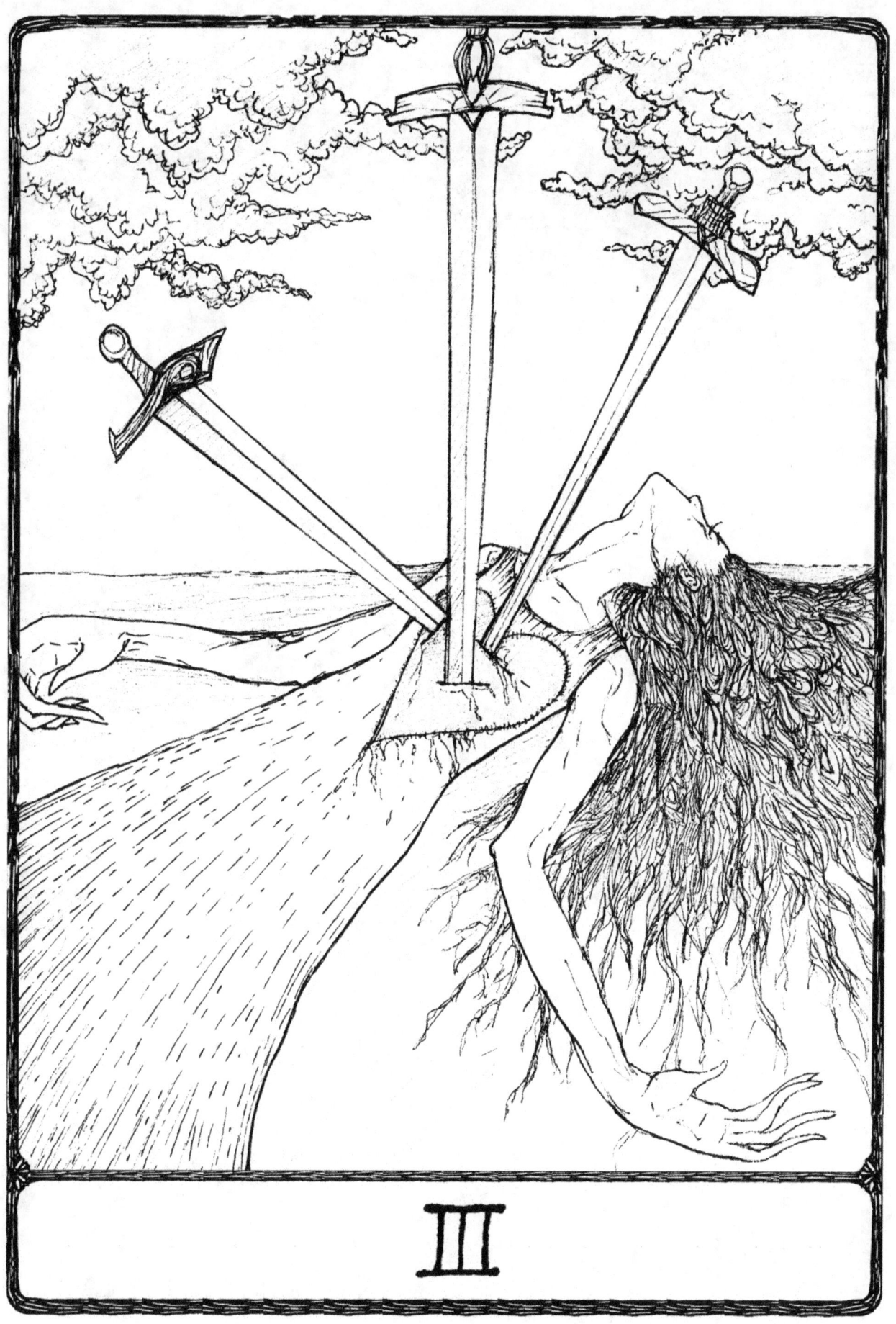

III

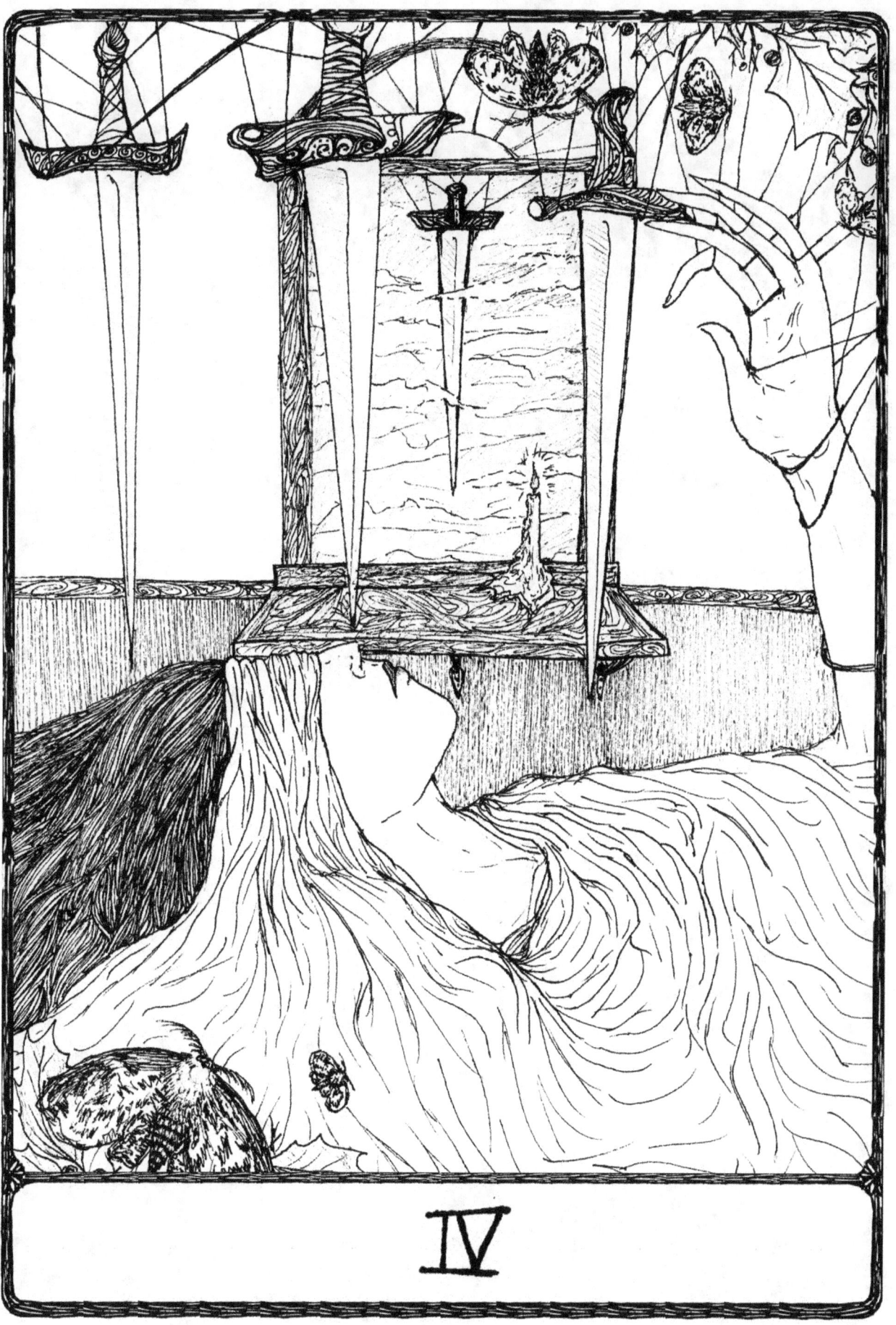

IV

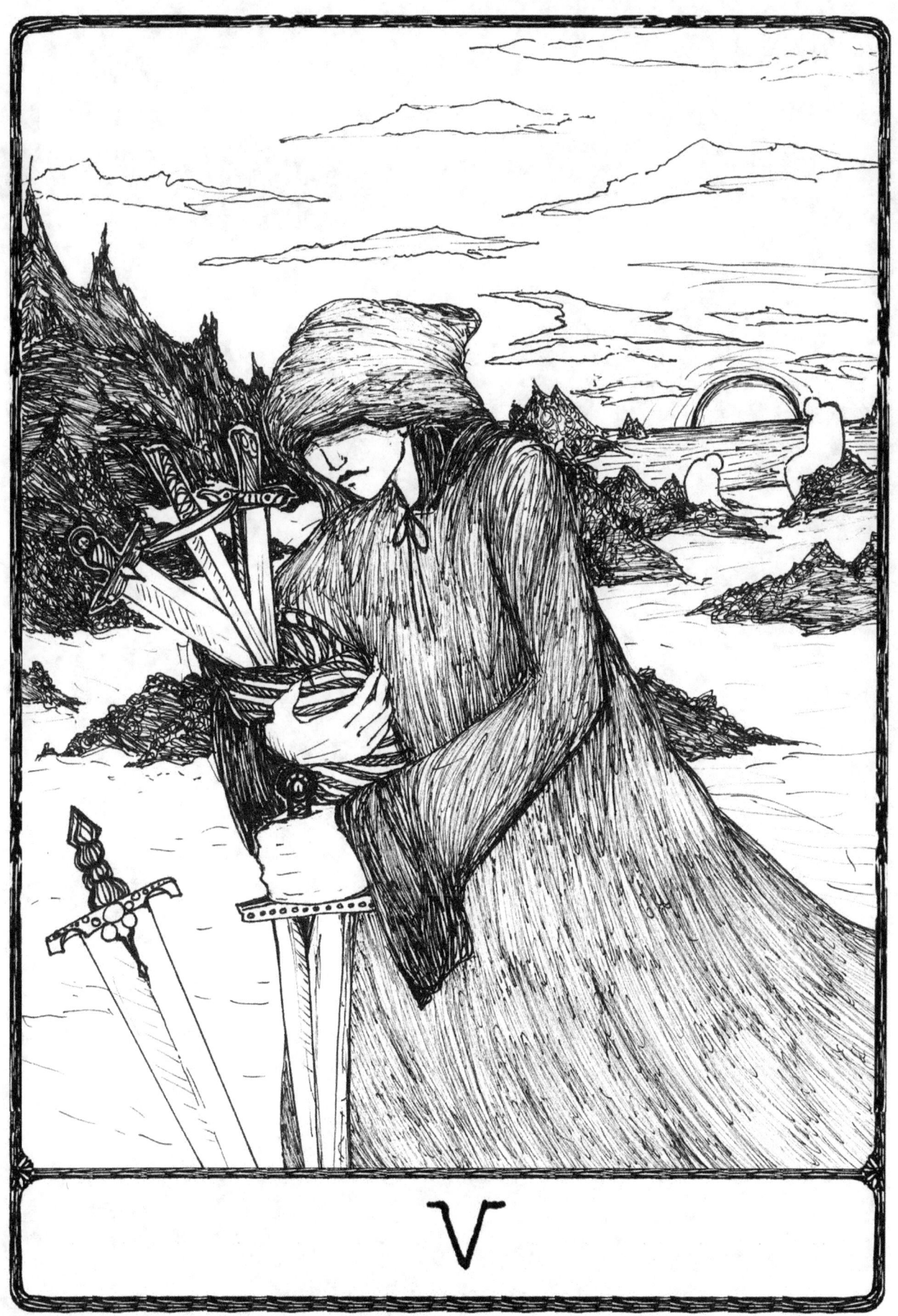

V

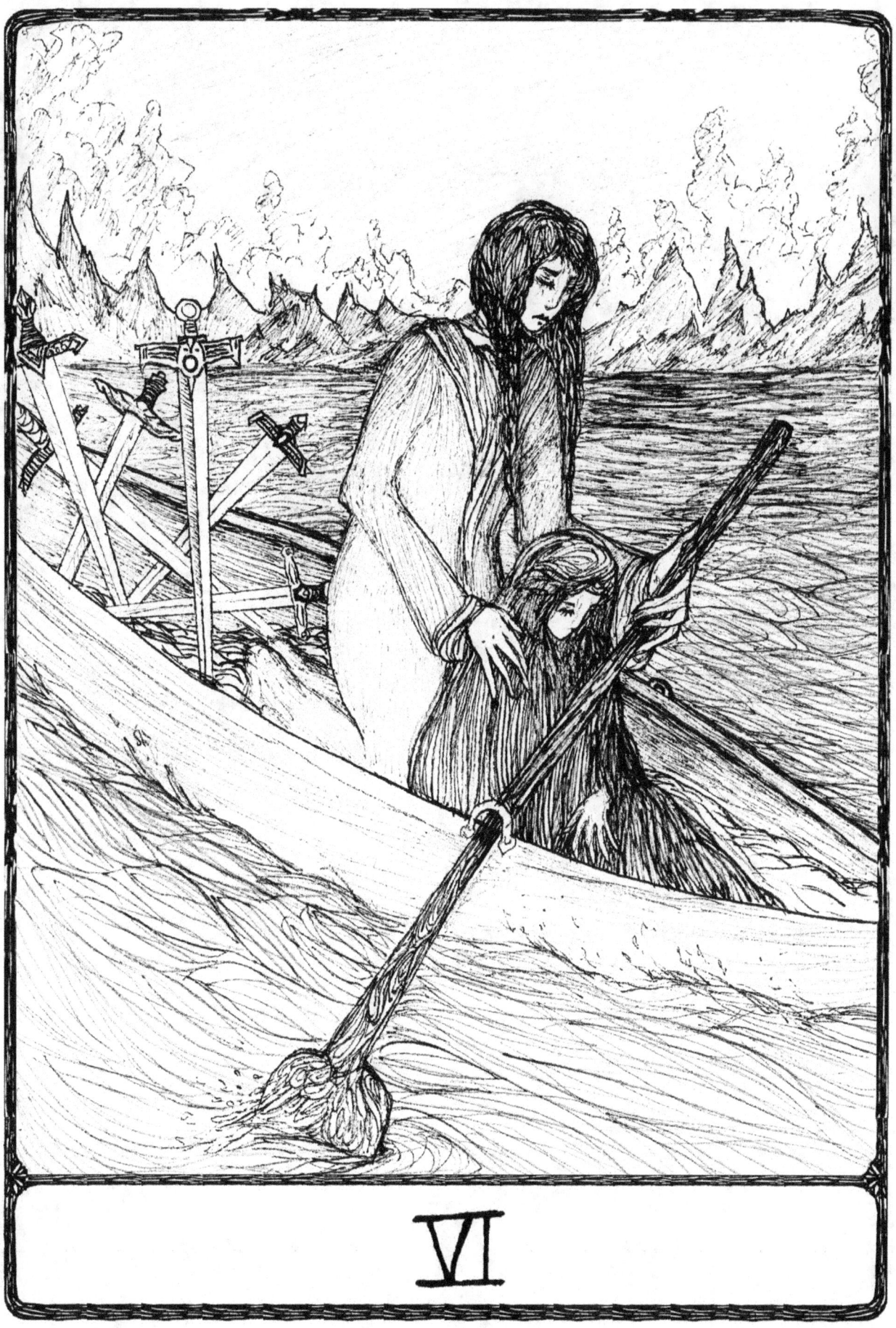

VI

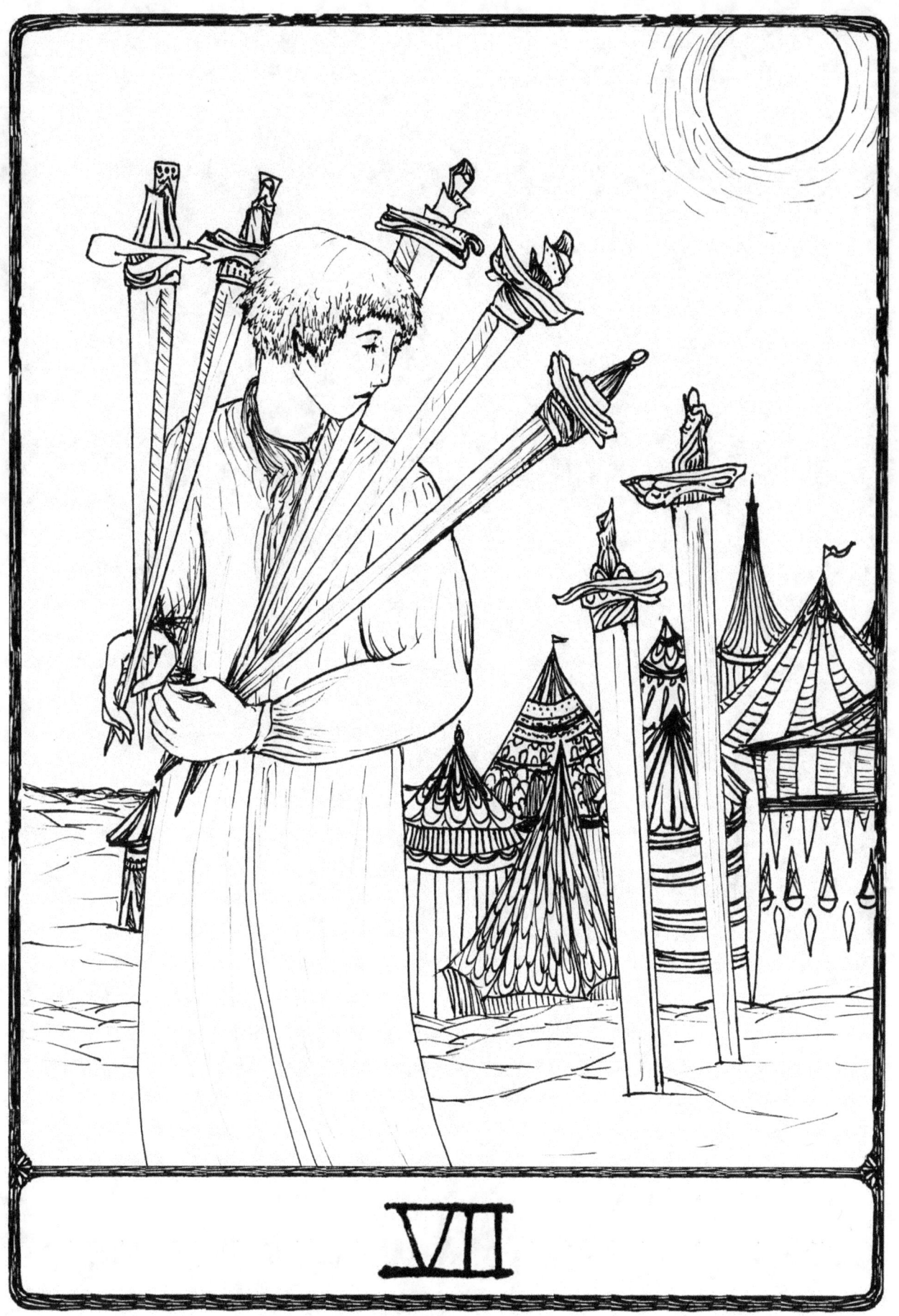

VII

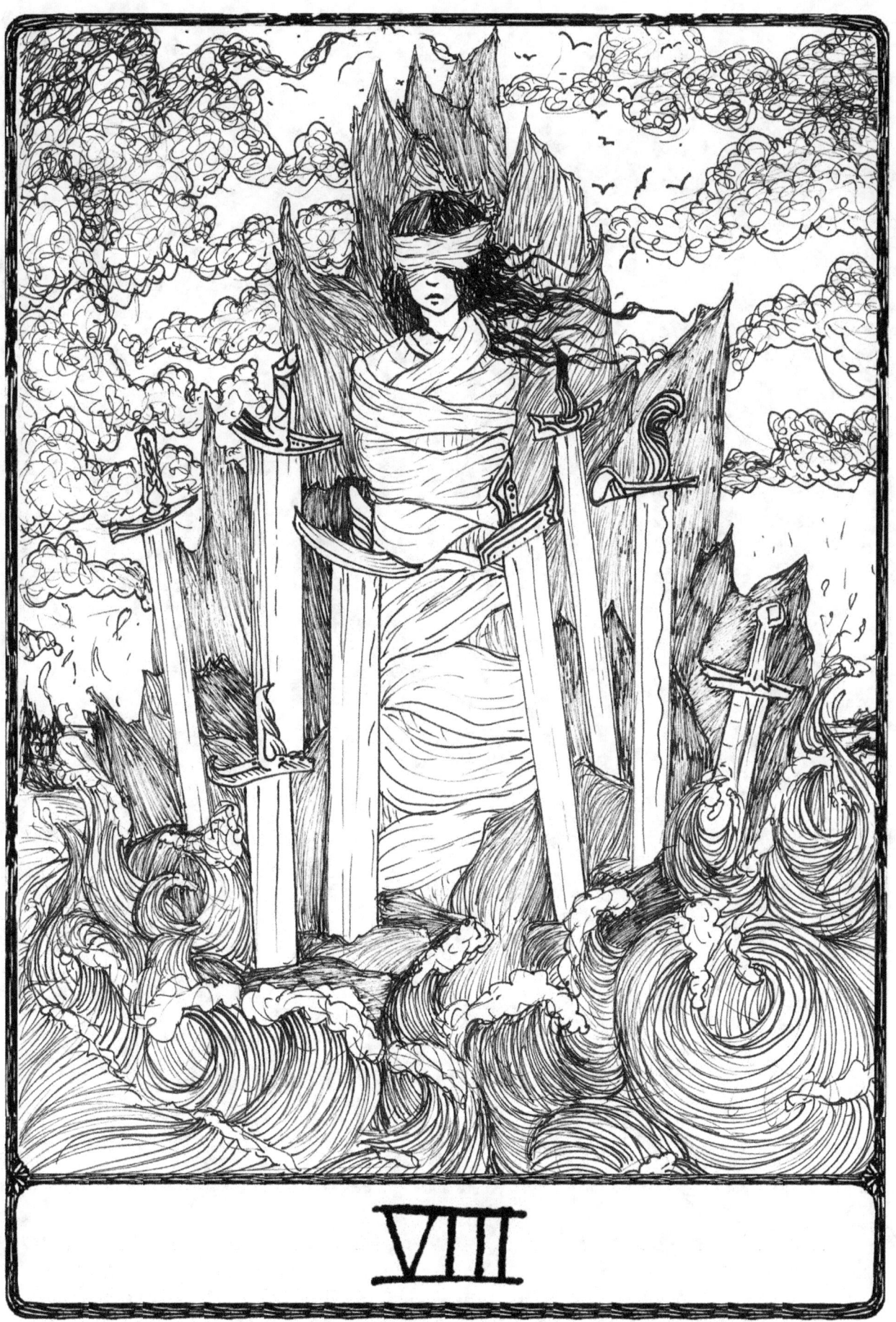

VIII

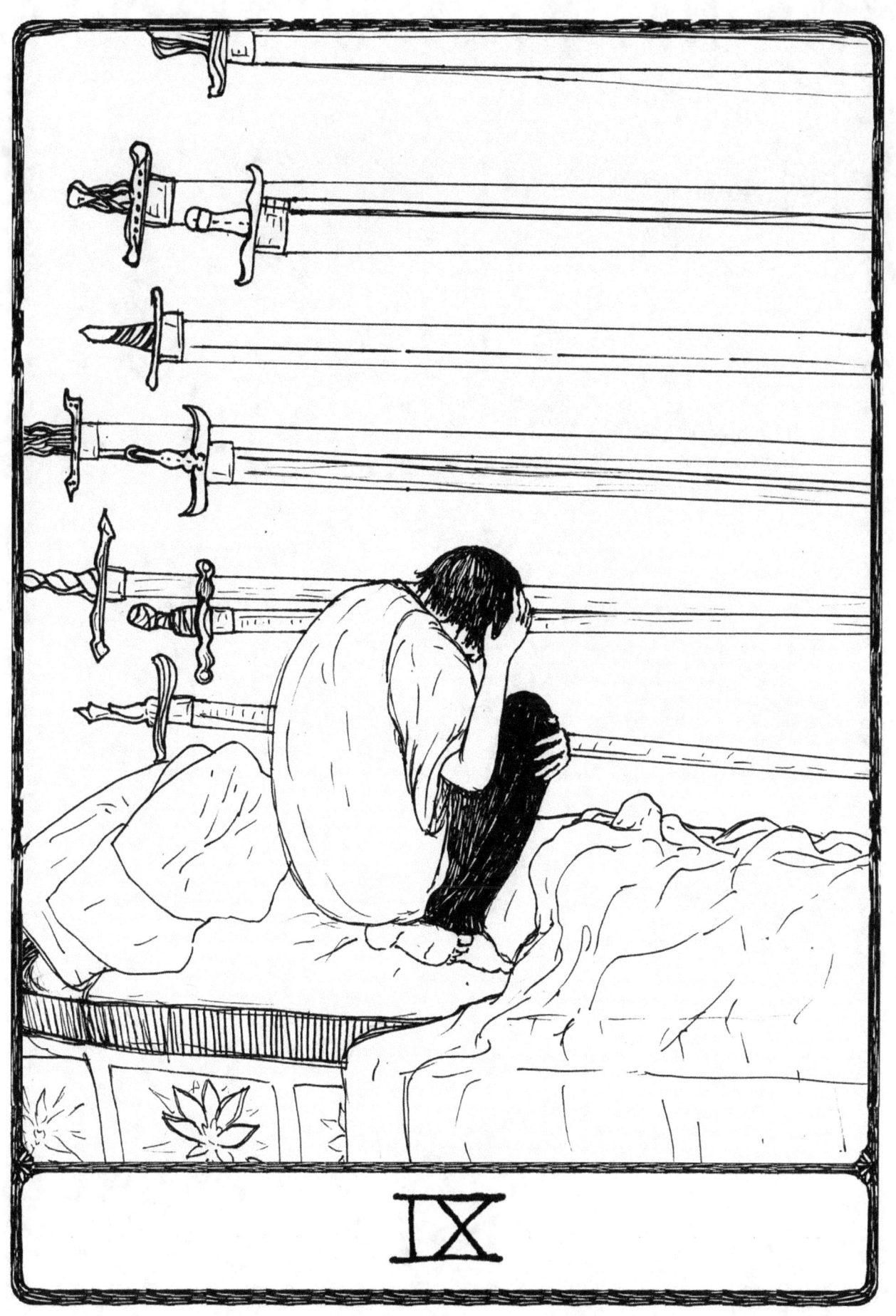

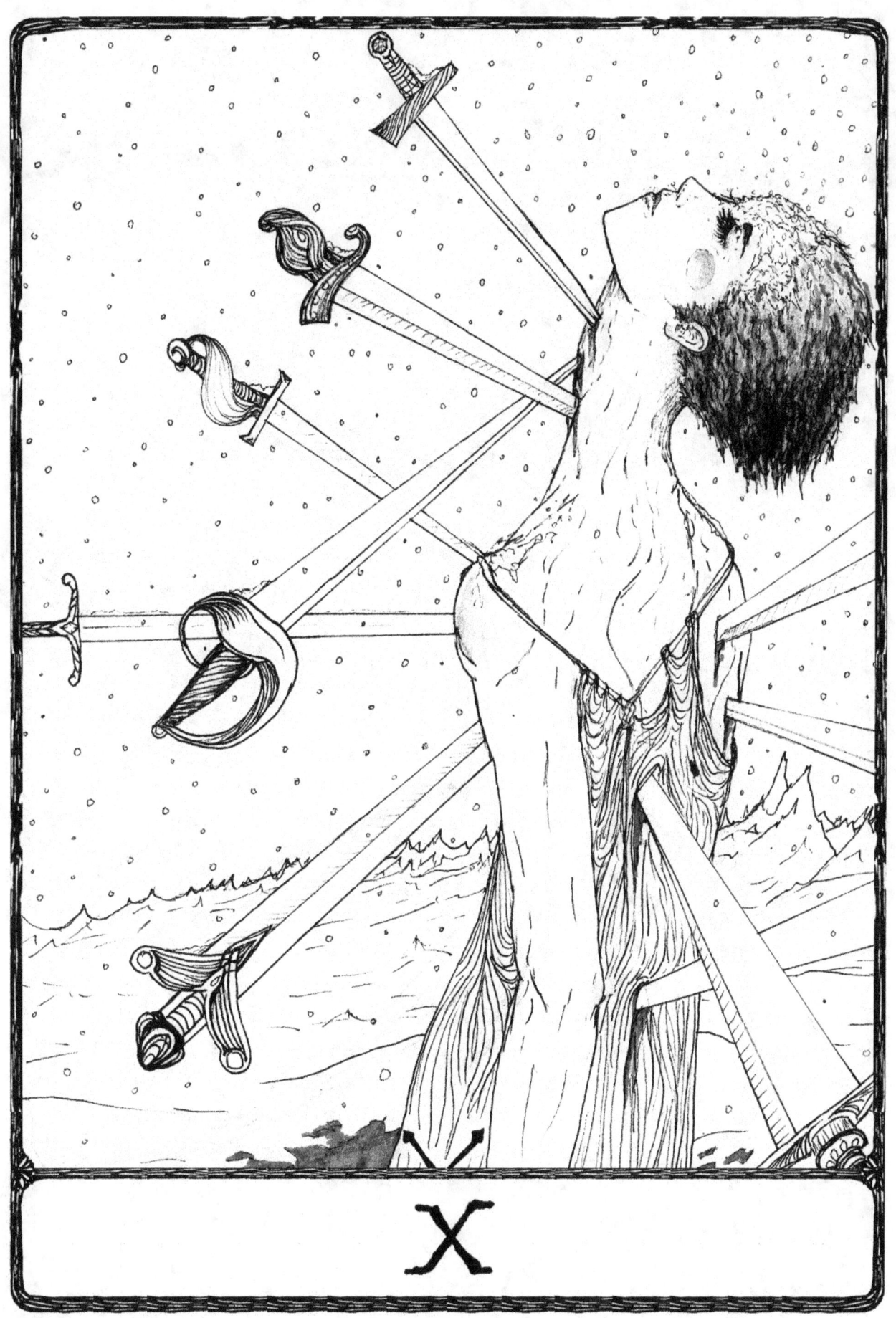

X

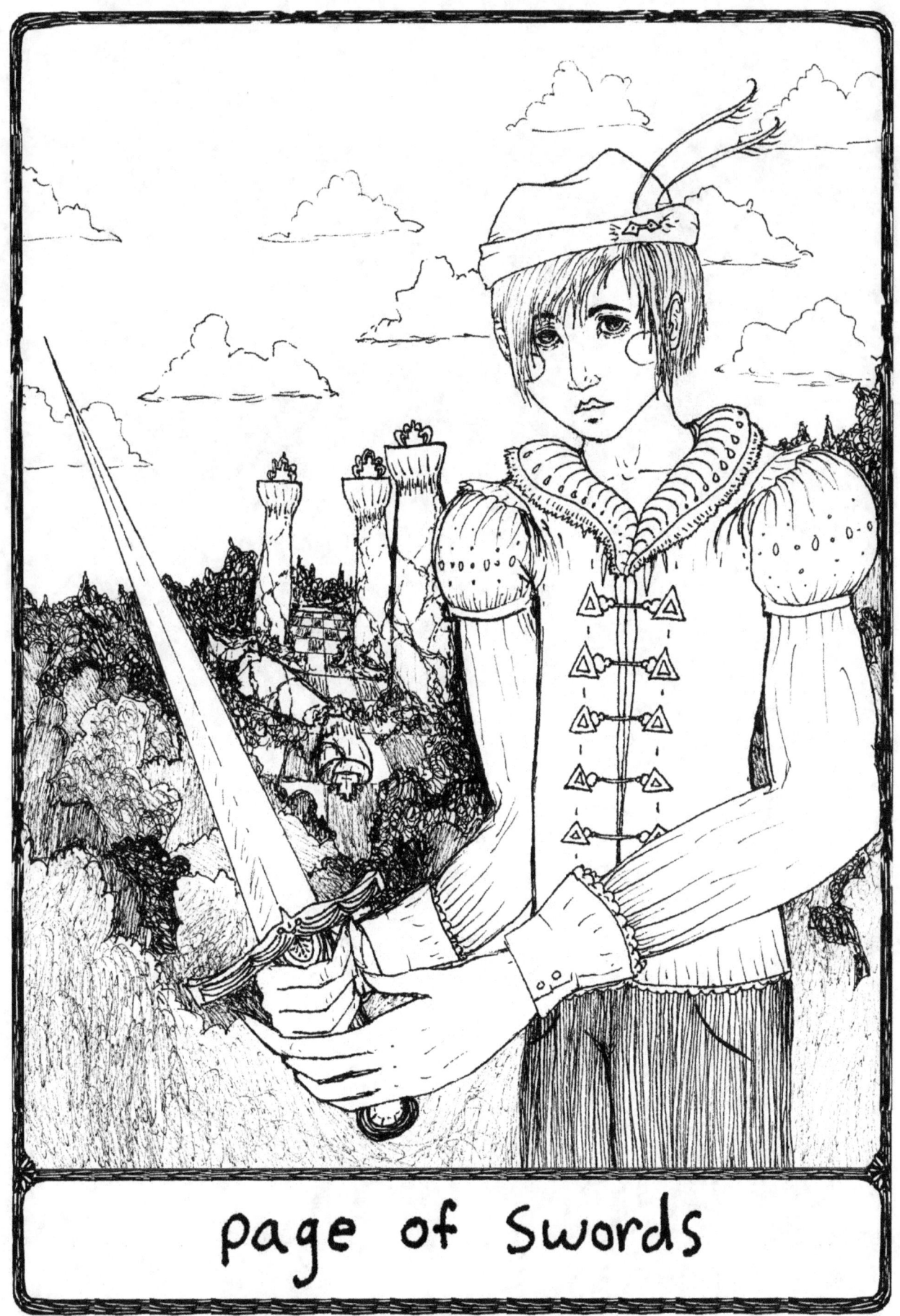

page of Swords

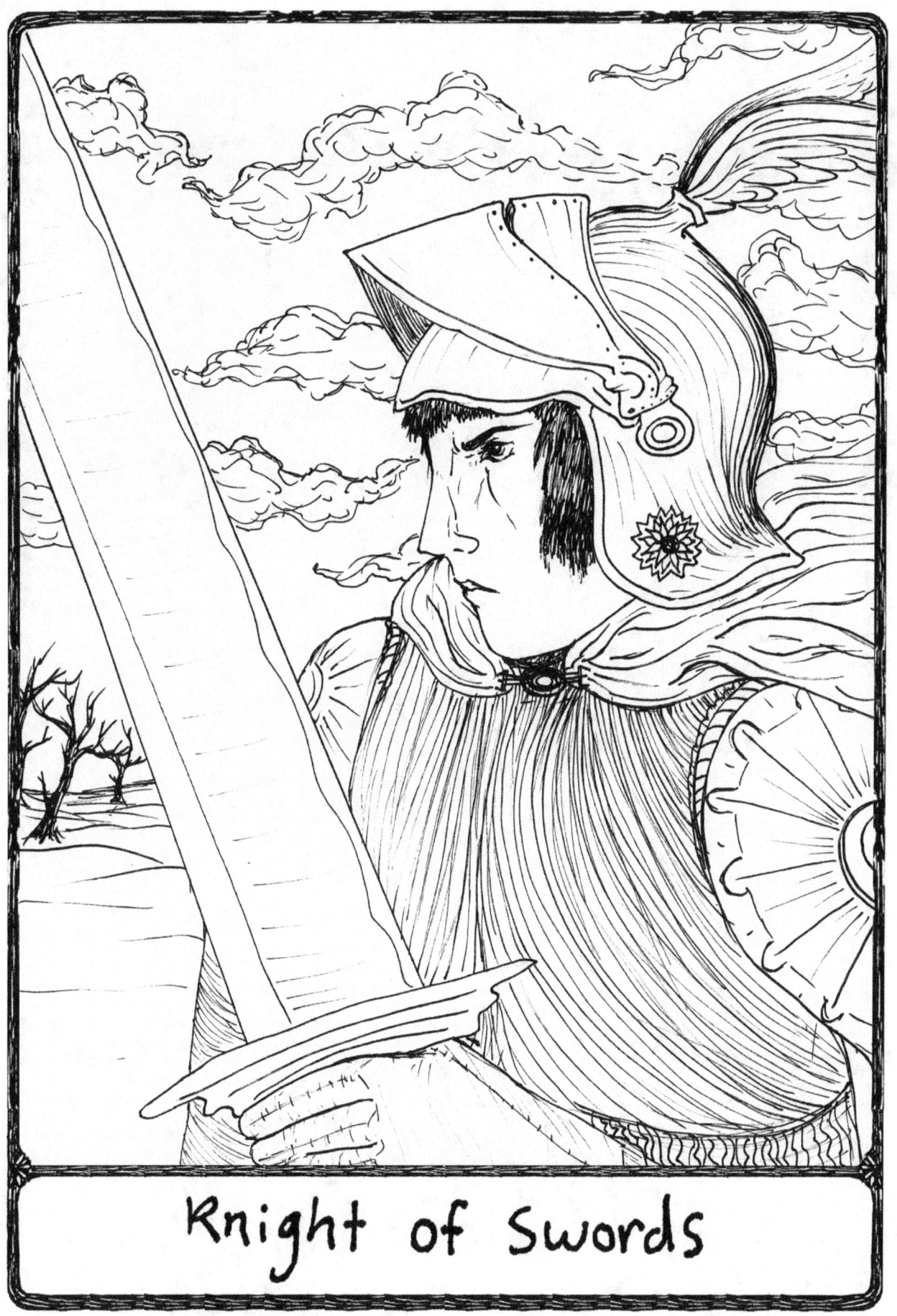

Knight of Swords

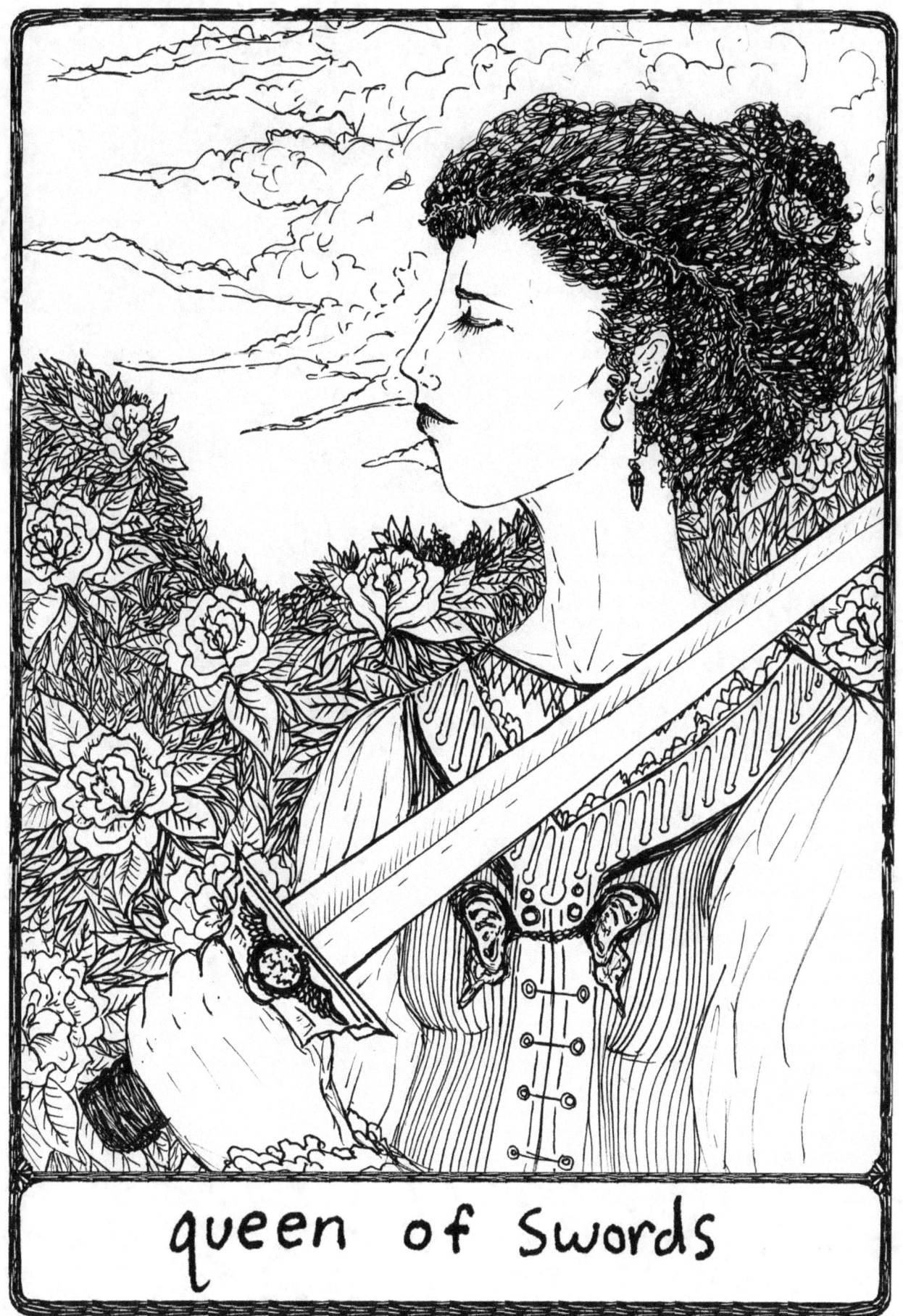

queen of Swords

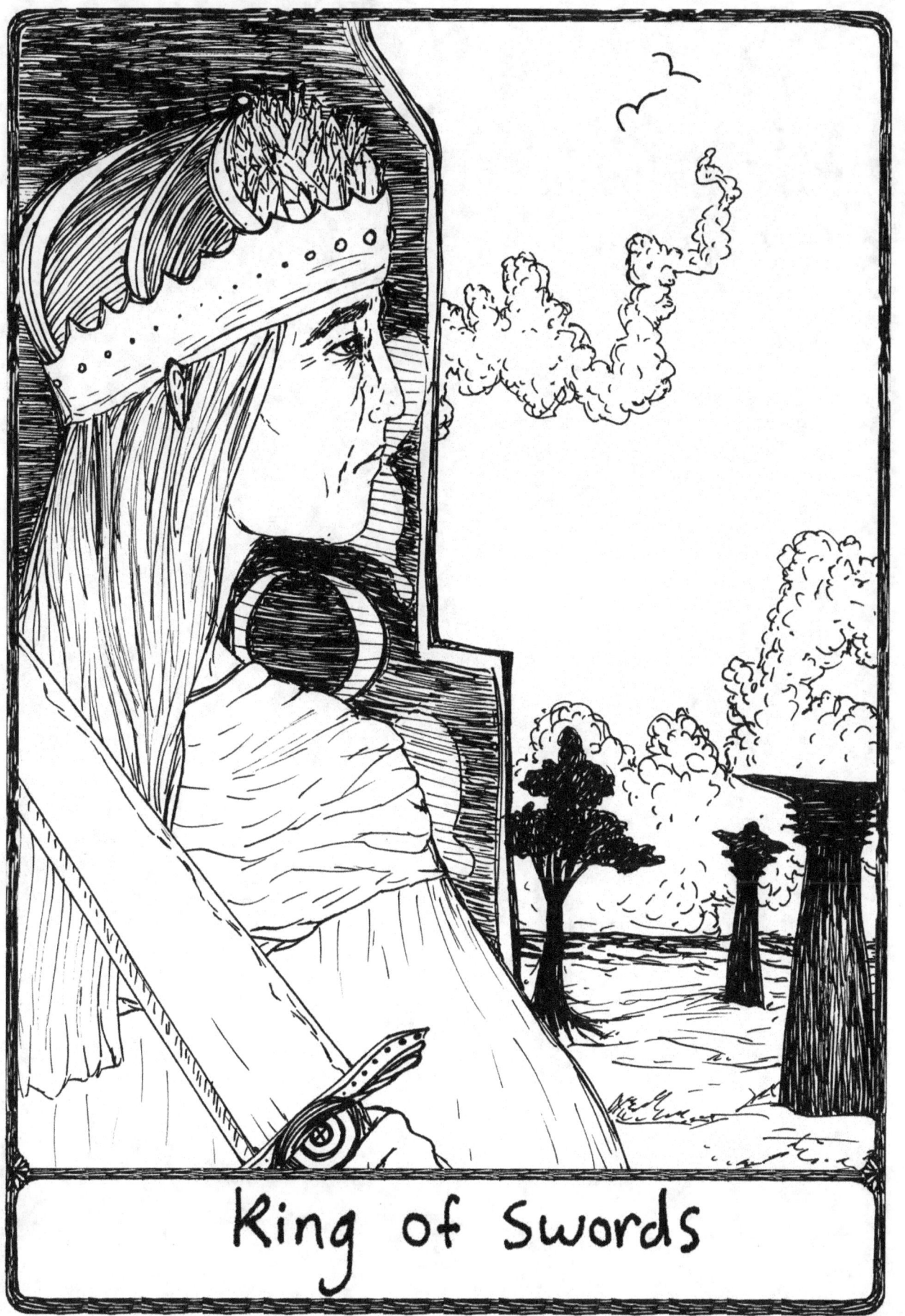

King of Swords

www.ingramcontent.com/pod-product-compliance
Lightning Source LLC
Chambersburg PA
CBHW081112180526

45170CB00008B/2817